REVOLUTION CUBAN STYLE

On a side wall of the great new dam at Contramaestre, Oriente, the following words are painted in huge letters:

"Los revolucionarios han de expresar sus ideas valientemente, definir sus principios y expresar sus intenciones para que nadie se engañe, ni amigo ni enemigo." Fidel Castro

"Revolutionaries must express their ideas valiantly, define their principles and state their intentions so that no one is deceived, neither friend nor foe."

REVOLUTION
CUBAN STYLE

Impressions of a Recent Visit

by GIL GREEN

INTERNATIONAL PUBLISHERS
New York

Library of Congress Catalog Card Number: 79-115170

Photographs by Mike Stein

SBN 7178-0263-9

Printed in the United States of America

Contents

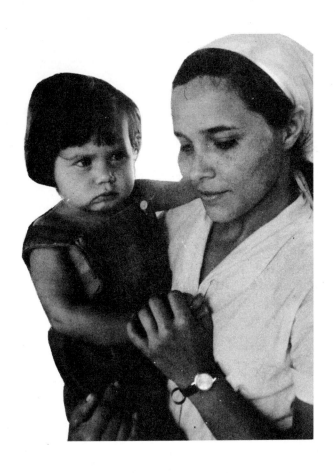

Director of a regional nursery, Oriente province.

Introduction

Ever since the triumph of the revolution in Cuba I had looked forward to the day I could visit that country. My eagerness to see the new Cuba did not arise from conflicting feelings about its revolution. I was passionately for it, heart and soul. I could truly say as did C. Wright Mills, "I am for the Cuban Revolution. I do not worry about it. I worry for it and with it."

But I wanted to see it for myself. I wanted to become intimately acquainted with how it was doing, its achievements and failings, the effects of the U.S.-imposed economic blockade, the problems and perspectives, and what this latest socialist revolution, right in our own front yard, had contributed to worldwide revolutionary experience.

The news of the *Granma* landing at Playas Coloradas in December 1956, reached me while I was a guest of the U. S. Government in its hostel in Leavenworth, Kansas. Later, while still a resident at this exclusive mansion, I read the fascinating interview with Fidel Castro by Herbert Matthews in *The New York Times*. This put to rest the stories of Castro's death. He was alive and well and fighting in the Sierra Maestra with his guerrilla army. It was in our walled compound, 40 feet high, that a number of us, including Puerto Rican nationalist political prisoners, jubilantly celebrated the victory of the rebellion on New Year's Day, 1959. And later, in April 1961, still living at government expense despite a specific law forbidding the use of federal funds for Communists, I suffered through the torturous hours of the Bay of Pigs invasion and shouted with joy at the news of its humiliating defeat.

But the opportunity to see Cuba did not come until ten years after the revolution had triumphed. I received an invitation at the end of April 1969. It did not take me many weeks to avail myself of this opportunity.

I spent three weeks in Cuba. I visited all of the six provinces and dozens of cities, towns and rural communities. I saw factories, farms, schools, hospitals and institutions. I interviewed scores of people and spent hours discussing my impressions and asking questions of prominent Cuban leaders.

But still three weeks is insufficient time fully to become acquainted with any place, and I make no claim to having become fully acquainted with Cuba. I recall the advice given me by a friend in Havana: "Do not depend upon first impressions, favorable or unfavorable. They could be misleading. Check impressions with facts and then double-check."

It would be presumptuous on my part to claim after so short a stay in Cuba that I could sift out all the superficial impressions from the more balanced judgments. Yet I learned so much from my visit to Cuba that I would consider my trip a wasteful indulgence if I did not share its rich experiences with others. I first began to write a number of articles for the press, then a pamphlet, and before I knew it these had grown into this little booklet.

Abstract objectivity about Cuba I cannot promise. I have already said that the Cuban Revolution is also my revolution. What I can promise is to attempt to remember the advice of my friend and where an impression cannot be checked out against fuller facts to make clear it is only an impression.

There is a wise old saying: "Never show a fool a job half done." Foes of revolutionary Cuba and of socialism in general would do well to remember this, for they see only the scaffolding, not the house rising up behind it. It also has meaning for revolutionary friends, who sometimes see through the scaffolding only the house they would like to see.

The Longest 90 Miles in the World

As Pan-Am flies, Cuba is only 90 miles from Key West and 1,350 miles from New York. But Pan-Am does not fly passenger planes to Cuba any more. Nor does any other airline out of the United States, except when planes are hijacked, a happening no longer rare.

I did not take the hijack route to Cuba. Mine was less imaginative, less dramatic and certainly less dangerous, even though considerably longer.

A ban on travel to Cuba was imposed by Washington soon after it became clear that the Cuban Revolution was not the usual Latin American palace upset. When neither Chase-Manhattan money nor U.S. military muscle could persuade the Cubans to abandon their revolutionary course, the time to get tough had come.

It was made a crime, punishable by loss of passport and possible imprisonment, for U.S. citizens to visit Cuba without a specific State Department seal of approval. Cuba was quarantined as if with the plague. A cruel, vindictive economic blockade was imposed, further tightened after the Bay of Pigs fiasco, and enforced by U.S. naval vessels prowling Cuban waters and by U.S. domination over satellite Latin American regimes.

On January 10, 1967, the ban on travel to Cuba was lifted by a new Supreme Court ruling. U.S. citizens could journey where they wished, so long as they did not use their passports to enter countries declared off-limits by the State Department. Cuba did not require passports from its visitors. It now became possible to visit Cuba legally whether Washington liked it or not.

There was one slight hitch. It meant travelling what must be the longest 90 miles in the world. To get to Cuba was relatively easy, even if somewhat longer and roundabout than a direct route. I went to Mexico City and from there flew via Cubana de Aviacion to Havana. But coming home was more complicated. Unable to prevent citizens from visiting Cuba, the State Department was still determined to make this as difficult as possible. The Mexican Government was ready to cooperate. It simply refused landing permits to U.S. citizens returning from Cuba whose passports did not bear an official State Department stamp, "Good for travel in Cuba."

Thus, I could come home only through Europe. I had to span the Atlantic two ways and journey some 12,000 miles round trip to visit an island not far off the coast of Florida.

1   Havana Libre

As I stepped off the plane at Havana Airport I had a strange feeling that I was really in San Juan, Puerto Rico, so similar was the clear, soft, balmy quality of breeze, the tropical fragrance and lush beauty of its multi-colored flora. This sensation was heightened by sighting in the distance an old friend whom I'd known in Puerto Rico. It was none other than *El Flamboyán*, the flamboyant tree, and well named it is indeed. It was in the season of its most lavish splendor, wearing a flaming orange-red mantle of a million petals. It is the peacock of trees.

I was to see *El Flamboyán* many times in Cuba — on Havana's wide avenues and lawns, along the highway to Camaguey, near cane fields in Oriente and tobacco fields in Pinar del Rio, and in the small mountain village of Mayari Arriba, where Raul Castro had been *comandante* of the 2nd Guerrilla Front. Wherever its brilliant colors caught my eye, I was reminded of Puerto Rico and of the common kinship and heritage of these two sister islands of the Antilles. Lola Rodríguez de Tío, the Puerto Rican poet, had captured this in a tender quatrain which compared Cuba and Puerto Rico to the two wings of a single bird, sharing a common heart.

I knew something about Puerto Rico, its history, and its continued colonial status. I found myself making constant comparisons between these two islands and their present status. It led to a greater appreciation of what the Cuban "experiment" means for all Latin America and particularly for the people of Puerto Rico.

After getting settled in my hotel room in the Havana Libre, formerly Hilton, I met a dark young man, Miguel Ángel Pérez Garcia, a student at the University of Havana and a gifted young linguist, assigned to me as guide and interpreter. I could get along reasonably well in Spanish, but a great deal depended on whom I was speaking with and how fast he threw the language in my direction. I took no chances, everytime I was unsure about what I heard I checked with Miguel. He was perfect, as both interpreter and guide, and an intelligent, pleasant companion as well.

A car was assigned for our use with a young blond, bushy-headed former teamster as our driver. Antonio was quiet and pensive, and worried over the car like a mother over a sick child.

There was good reason for this. The car was somewhat older than the revolution and had seen better days. It was one of the more desirable cars around, for Cuba is not spending its hard-earned foreign exchange, nor using up foreign credits, to buy passenger cars; not yet anyway. Priority goes to other more essential machines and motor vehicles, like trucks, tractors and buses.

To set out by car was an adventure. Antonio would check the tires, race the engine to feel the pulse of his patient, and every time the latter would wheeze or cough it would be like a tear at Antonio's heart. But the car had its advantages. No one could possibly know where, when or why it would break down. As it had a propensity for doing so quite regularly, and the perversity to choose the exact spot in which the particular missing or ailing part could not be replaced or repaired, it added both spice and meat to the journey. I was able to see people and places I would not have seen otherwise.

My first days in Havana were spent roaming the streets, watching the people, gaping at store windows, visiting *El Cordón de la Habana,* the green belt, and trying to catch the mood and spirit of the people and the contour and soul of the city.

Havana is a large modern city of over a million inhabitants. It wraps around an immense natural harbor, one of the very best in the world, and then lazily stretches along miles of sea coast on the Gulf of Mexico. It has a number of ultra-modern skyscrapers and many solidly built, closer to earth, 18th and 19th-century Spanish colonial structures.

The Havana Libre is located in the main hotel and night life area of the city, with many restaurants, theaters and night clubs. Like the Condado section of San Juan, it used to be the main tourist district, with gambling and prostitution widespread. Today it is still an amusement center, where people go for a good time, a movie or a restaurant, but it has lost its casinos, its prostitution, and most of the former gaudy neon light raucousness.

None of the streets of the city are as brightly lit as they formerly were. Some are quite dim. This is a matter not of policy, but of necessity. It is one of the effects of the U.S.-imposed economic blockade, which prevents Cuba from buying her gas and fuel oil from the nearby Gulf region, compelling her instead to have her oil shipped from across the ocean by a fleet of Soviet tankers.

Along the highways of Cuba are huge, solid-black billboards. As we approached we saw a small white square in the center. As we got still closer we distinguished letters inside the square and then finally could spell out the word CLIC. Nothing more. On the bottom of the poster, beneath the blackness, there was a curt reminder to turn off lights when not needed, to save fuel oil. It was a striking poster with its stark simplicity.

We saw other similar reminders of what the blockade has meant. Every time our car broke down there were curses about the damned Yankee imperialists, for had there been GM spare parts much of our trouble could have been easily avoided or overcome.

Everyone in Havana knows why the streets are dimly lit and who to blame for this. And everyone in Cuba knows from where and at what great effort come the gas and oil to run their machines and to keep their economy going and growing. The Cubans have learned to improvise and to make their own spare parts, and their geologists, with aid from other socialist countries, are finding their own natural oil and peat resources.

Among my first impressions of the people on the streets of Havana was the completely natural way in which white and black persons mingled. Youngsters on their way to school or frolicking in the park, people at restaurants or ice cream parlors, youth on their way to a movie or night spot, were nearly always both black and white. When I mentioned this to Miguel he seemed surprised that I found this worthy of comment. He had read about racism in the United States, about ghettos, discrimination, segregation, yet he found it difficult to visualize a society in which acceptance of color difference was not the most natural thing in the world. No matter where we went in Cuba, not once did I see the suspicion, tension, animus and artificiality that so frequently characterizes white-black relations in the United States.

2   Comparing Two Cities

Having flown to Havana from Mexico City it was natural to make a comparison between these two cities and their peoples. The last time I had visited Mexico City was 30 years before. It has expanded tremendously since then, altered much, and yet remained basically the same. Walking the streets of Mexico City, I was left with the impression of a city bulging with people. I saw fewer barefooted persons than in the 1930s, but there were still all too many. Indian peasant women carrying babes wrapped around their midriffs were to be seen everywhere. Barefoot, listless, often with tiny tots grouped around them in tattered clothes, they would sit on the sidewalk propped up against a wall, or lie curled in deep sleep, their meager wares spread beside them.

Havana's streets were in striking contrast to this. They too were frequently very crowded, but not as if they city were bursting at the seams with a teeming humanity that seemed to have nowhere to go. Havana's pedestrians were better dressed and far cleaner and neater in appearance. I saw no one barefoot, not even children at play. I saw no people sitting or sleeping on sidewalks. I saw no beggars, although Mexico City is filled with them, many of whom are street urchins.

I was told there are no beggars or people without shoes in Cuba, but I can only speak for what I saw. I saw none in Havana and one in the other cities and towns I visited, not Santa Clara, Camaguey, Cienfuegos, Ciego de Avila, Holguín, Gíbara, Bayamo, Santiago de Cuba, Pinar del Rio, nor any other community I visited.

Moreover, while I had seen many a *borrachón* on the streets of Mexico City, I saw no drunkards on the streets of Havana and only one in the three weeks spent in Cuba.

I mentioned this absence of *borrachos* to Miguel and Antonio after we had spent about two weeks traveling together. They both laughed and assured me that there were some and that they would scrounge one up for me. Sure enough a few days later, at a small place called Herradura, where our car insisted on making one of its unscheduled stops, a Cuban drunk did stagger by us. My two companions immediately took credit for this find, but I felt that the car was more deserving of it.

One contrast between Mexico City and Havana would seem to belie my impression about people in Havana being better dressed and on the whole better off than those in Mexico City. The stores in Mexico City were crammed with merchandise piled ceiling high. The stores in Havana looked quite bare, with little to display and little to sell.

In Mexico City one could buy just about anything if, of course, one had the money. In Havana and everywhere else in Cuba people seemed to have the money but nearly everything was tightly rationed. This was particularly true of food and clothing.

Thus if one were to judge by the stores alone there would seem to be *prima facie* evidence that the people of Mexico City were living in plush prosperity, while the people of Havana were starved and naked.

Discussing this contrast with Cubans I usually got the same kind of reply. Typical was what one man said to me in the city of Pinar del Rio: "Down the block you will see a butcher shop. It is now afternoon and all its meat is gone. Before the revolution there never was a meat shortage in that store. But the majority of the people in this neighborhood hardly ever ate meat. They didn't have the money. They lived on rice and beans. Today everyone eats meat; true, not enough, but for the majority far more than yesterday. Some of us may eat less than before, but think of all those who eat a great deal more."

A pamphlet published by the Catholic University students Association in Havana in 1956, three years *before* the rebel armies marched into Havana, gave statistical evidence for this assertion. According to this report, 96 per cent of farmers and agricultural workers usually ate no meat, only one per cent ate fish, only 2.1 per cent ate eggs, and only 11.2 per cent drank milk.*

Certainly, if all the people on the streets of Mexico City suddenly had the money to buy the things they needed, store shelves would be barer than a field invaded by locusts. Yet this is not a fully satisfactory explanation for the continued existence of shortages in Cuba. In defending what is now, as against what was, there is no intention to make a virtue of empty shelves and rationing. Rationing is necessary to guarantee that some do not get more than their share and others less. But anyone, who has had to wait his turn in line to buy things he needs, detests doing so and looks forward to the day when it will no longer be necessary.

Why an Agrarian Reform, published in Spanish by Agrupacion Catolica Universitaria, Havana, 1956.

3.   Shortages and Rationing

Miguel's mother, a laundry worker, supplied the facts that gave me an insight into what rationing means in concrete human terms. Each person living in Havana is entitled to three-quarters of a pound of meat, three eggs and one pound of rice weekly. Bread is rationed at three-quarters of a pound per person per day. A liter of fresh milk a day is rationed to children under seven years of age and to old people over 65. Others get three cans of condensed milk a month. Fresh fruit, vegetables and canned goods frequently are hard to come by and rationing varies with the supply on hand.

Fish, on the other hand, is unrationed. Strange as it may seem, and certainly contrary to what I had assumed, the Cuban people are not great fish *aficianados*. They had never cultivated a taste for it. Yet Cuba with over 2,000 miles of coastline is surrounded by the sea and its adjacent waters are world famous for their fishing grounds.

Before the revolution fishing was done mainly with rod and reel. Small fishing vessels also operated out of sea coast hamlets and supplied fish mainly for their own locales. Deep-sea fishing was a gentleman's sport, attracting many North American enthusiasts. Pre-revolutionary Cuba did not possess adequate transportation and refrigeration facilities. Thus the people in the large cities and in the interior rural areas rarely ate fish.

Hemingway's old man of the sea was a single, solitary fisherman, engaged in a personal vendetta with the briny deep and its more ferocious species of marine life. He was not part of a larger struggle to make the sea yield up the rich protein food with which to feed an undernourished Cuban population.

The revolution came and this changed. Fishing cooperatives were organized; storage refrigerators, dry-docks and shipyards built; and a large commercial fishing fleet established. Already in 1965 there were 31 fishing cooperatives with 9,500 fishermen and four thousand fishing boats. Fish production had increased from 1,300 metric tons in 1959 to 15,500 metric tons — an increase of over 1,000 per cent in six years' time. In 1963, Cuba's fishing fleet totaled 4,556 tons, in 1969, 56,840 tons. So today seafood is more plentiful and the Cuban people are acquiring a taste for it. But even now fish is not the most popular of dishes, thus its exclusive non-rationed status.

Rationing is supplemented in a number of ways, however. Most important of all is the system of people's dining halls, conveniently located to serve the people in factories, offices, schools and institutions. At these supplementary dining rooms a complete midday meal is sold for 50 to 60 cents. This meal consists of soup or beans; fish, meat or eggs; bread, beverage and dessert. In most schools lunches are free. For retired people, and where working people are home because they work nights, neighborhood peoples' restaurants serve the same kind of meals. Where factories are near residential communities, the same communal dining rooms serve both. Thus most people are guaranteed one ration-free meal a day.

There are also many restaurants in Havana of varying quality and price range where people can buy dinner without regard to rationing. The Mar-Init chain of sea food restaurants provides meals at extremely reasonable prices, but cheapest and most popular are the pizzerias.

Restaurant eating doubtless favors those with higher earnings. However, my impression is that money is not a major obstacle to dining out. With a shortage of goods, working people have extra pesos in their pockets. There are exceptions to this, of course, especially in families with a number of children and only one breadwinner.

The greatest obstacle is getting into a restaurant, especially the better ones. So great is the demand that it is necessary to make reservations in advance. The offices of some of these open as early as six in the morning, so that workers on their way to work can make reservations for that evening. The reservation has to be for a definite hour so that the restaurant can accommodate the largest number of diners. When dining out must be planned in this way, it tends to reduce the frequency of restaurant eating. In other cities the problem is not the same. We ate in many restaurants at which there was no crowding or waiting line and no reservations were required.

I was also told that families in Havana who had relatives on the land supplement their food stock with fresh produce brought in to them. Thus people are by no means hungry or even undernourished. But rationing is not fun.

Clothes rationing is also strict and with less possibilities for supplementation. However, the clothing of Cubans is simpler than the clothing of people living in colder climates. It is even simpler than for the people of Mexico. There, the high plateaus and mountain ranges bring sharp and sudden variations in weather.

Between day and night, the temperature can fall swiftly from a tropical high to a frigid low.

With Cuba's warm, balmy climate all year around, and with only a slight fall in night temperature, heavy clothing is an encumbrance. Heavy shoes, galoshes, woolen suits or dresses, winter overcoats or even fall topcoats, are unnecessary. Only when Miguel and I went to the La Tropicana night club one evening did either of us wear a jacket.

Men usually dress in lightweight slacks and colorful sport shirts. Women wear light, colorful frocks that are simply yet tastefully and stylishly cut to enhance natural body lines. Cubans, by the way, men as well as women, are fastidious about their appearance. Castro may wear what looks like a shaggy beard, but I found to my surprise that practically all Cuban men are well-groomed and that among major service industries of Cuba are the *peluquerías* and *barberías*. There are nearly as many *barberías* for men as *peluquerías* for women. Women's magazines carry items about clothes, with patterns for home sewing and many families make their own clothes, as cloth by the yard is more plentiful and cheaper than the ready-made garments.

I was told that everyone is entitled to a basic, minimum quantity of clothing and that rationing is structured on this base, replacing or adding to it. For men this includes three pairs of trousers, six shirts, and a comparable quantity of socks, underclothes, etc. Each family has a group number assigned to it and goes shopping only when it is its number's turn, avoiding a situation in which everyone tries to buy things at the same time. Placards in store windows and notices in the press inform the people which group's turn it is and on what day the next changeover will take place.

A notice appeared recently in *Granma*, the official newspaper of the Communist Party, informing the public that for a three-day period all groups could shop at the same time so that families that had missed their original turns could make up for them. Thus, the basic needs of the people seem to be met and certain guarantees are established against selfish hoarding.

Aware of shortages and rationing I tried to discern signs of black market activities. Usually these manifest themselves when sharpies, hanging around hotels where foreigners live, try to buy foreign clothes or sell national currency below the official rate of exchange. My own personal Geiger counter found no evidence of such activities.

The Cuban press reports black marketeering of some sorts. Yet other foreigners I spoke with also found no evidence of such activities.

4   The Year of the Decisive Effort

"You have come at the right time," I was told upon arriving in Havana. "The island is hopping with activity. You will see much. You have certainly come at the right time." For me, any time would have been the "right time" to come to revolutionary Cuba. But I soon found out what was meant.

Ever since Fidel and his *barbudos* made "Cuba *libre*" more than the name of a drink, every year has been given its own designated name, emphasizing a special thrust. Thus, 1959 was the year of liberation; 1960, the year of agrarian reform; 1961, the year of education, when the massive assault on illiteracy took place. Later, 1967 became the year of solidarity with Vietnam; 1968, the year of the heroic guerrilla, and 1969 was named, "The Year of the Decisive Effort." It has also been referred to as "The Year of 18 Months." This latter designation led me to chide Cuban friends that their revolution had already accomplished the impossible; it had added six months to the year.

The "decisive effort" is economic. Its objective is to push the country over the hump, so to speak, especially to put an end to the yearly foreign trade deficit and to ground its longer range plans for economic development in a sound foundation.

The concentration is on agriculture. This is so much the case that I found rare mention of industries not directly related to agriculture. In this respect there seems to have been a swing from the main stress in the first years of the revolution.

It is now recognized that overcoming underdevelopment in Cuba does not mean putting manufacturing first and agriculture second. Because of Cuba's extremely fertile soil and nearly perfect growing climate, and especially because there is a socialist world and the possibility of some rational division of labor, it is not necessary for Cuba to imitate the other socialist countries and try to produce the very same products. As Fidel has stressed in his speeches, the rapid growth of world population and the general world trend toward urbanization create an ever greater world need for agricultural products.

"Cuba may not for a long time, or ever, produce its own jet plane, but why does it have to if it can get them made more efficiently and cheaply elsewhere? But how many countries in the world can have three crops a year? Cuba can. With that Cuba can industrialize gradually, modernize and mechanize her agriculture, rapidly raise the living standards of her people, their education, culture and leisure, and put an end to under-development once and for all. The key for us is agri-culture."

If this was said to me once, it was said to me a dozen times. The words differed; the meaning was the same.

There are two sides to this year's decisive effort: the short-range and the long-range. Both mesh closely together and are interdependent. The single main short-range objective is the production of ten million tons of sugar cane in the 1970 harvest. What this means as an effort can be grasped better when it is recalled that only four times in Cuban history, and only twice since the revolution, did the sugar harvest go above six million tons, and only once did it reach a total of 7.2 million tons. The 1969 harvest, however, was some-what below five million tons. The objective is to double sugar production in one year's time, a herculean task.

The longer-range plan has to do with diversification of agriculture, gradual industrialization, and with what is known in Cuba as "the struggle for eternal spring."

When I first arrived in Cuba I was quite skeptical about the realizability of the goal of ten million tons of sugar. It did not seem realistic to me, especially as I knew that less ambitious objectives for sugar increases in previous years had not been realized. How then could sugar cane production be doubled in one year? But by the time I left the island I too had been carried away by the mass enthusiasm and mass determination that, come what may, this goal must be reached.

Everywhere I went in Cuba I saw posters on build-ings and billboards, banners along highways, slogans

This typical roadside billboard relays the motto of the Year of the Decisive Effort, "Everyone Ready for the 10 Million."

painted on factory walls, articles in the press day by
day, stressing this sugar cane goal. The words "10
VAN" leap at you everywhere. This slogan means that
ten million tons are on their way. This goal is so important an objective that it is seen as the great revolutionary exploit for today and constantly compared with
the Moncada Barracks assault in 1953 and the *Granma*
landing of Fidel and his guerrilla band in December
1956. The entire prestige of the leadership, from Fidel
down, and the honor of the revolution itself has been
placed at stake in the struggle for *los diez millones*.

I met one individual who was bitterly critical of the
leadership for its lack of planning ability and of Cubans
in general for their sloppiness in organizational matters and inability to stick to hard back-breaking tasks.
This man, who had been in Cuba for a number of years
as an industrial efficiency expert, said that the Cubans
were hopeless when it came to organized, sustained efforts and that it would take three generations to change
this. Yet my conviction is that Cuba will reach its 1970
sugar goal or come mighty close to it. I have an exceedingly high regard for mass revolutionary zeal, but
my opinion is based on more tangible evidence. Everywhere I went I not only found enthusiasm for the sugar
goal, but much of it harnessed to carefully planned, organized efforts to achieve the objective.

In Cienfuegos, for example, not far from Playa Girón
(Bay of Pigs), we visited an ultra-modern, completely
mechanized, sugar-loading dock and granary with a
capacity of 90,000 tons. Railroad cars and motor trucks
mechanically dumped their contents of golden sugar
granules onto moving conveyer belts that carried them
into the storehouse and from there directly into the
holds of waiting ships. This combination loading dock

and warehouse had just been built. Before, hundreds of men toiled from 15 to 20 days to load a ship of 15,000 tons. Now a handful of men can load the same ship mechanically in 12 hours. Everything was under switchboard touch control. This enterprise was built with an eye to the 1970 sugar harvest. It is planned to keep the conveyer belts moving and to load ships 24 hours a day, seven days a week.

In Santa Clara, the geographic heart of the island, we visited machine building plant, Fábric Águilar Noriega. This is the most modern, and largest iron-smelting and machine-building plant in Cuba. It has 1,700 workers of whom 200 are women, and operates on a three-shift basis. We found it busily engaged in making machine parts for the sugar mills in the expectation of a much greater demand when the wear and tear of the new harvest begins. More important, the plant was working on the production of combines and mechanical cane-cutters, the first of which were to be put into use in time for the 1970 harvest. The aim was to turn out 28 sugar-harvesting combines of the *Libertadora* type and 325 cane-cutting machines of the Henderson type. Everything in the plant was attuned to one goal — to help provide the tools, parts and machines for the big year.

In Bayamo, in Oriente province, we visited a new textile plant for the production of sacks. When finished this plant will be one of the largest of its kind in the world. Already 500 workers, 81 per cent of whom are women, were at work producing twine and weaving sacks. The mill will employ 1,300 workers when completed. It is being rushed so that it can have sacks ready for that portion of the 1970 crop that is refined and shipped in sacks.

In Camaguey province, at Ciego de Avila, we visited
one of the largest sugar mills, El Central Venezuela.
The men were just finishing the milling of the 1969 harvest and the air was filled with the sweet, pungent odor
of fermenting sugar. But the workers were not preparing to leave the mill for work elsewhere as was previously the case when the *zafra* (harvest) was over.
They were merely switching work assignments at the
mill itself. Already an imposing new addition had aris-
en, built by construction workers while the milling was
taking place. Now would come the work of installing
the new, more modern milling machinery, and cleaning,
repairing and replacing parts on the older sections. El
Central Venezuela aimed to double its milling capacity
in time for the bonanza harvest.

Traditionally, sugar mill workers faced unemployment and hardship once the milling season was over
and the "dead season" began. They would leave their
communities and roam from town to town searching
for work, any work, and often at wages considerably
below those received at the sugar mills. This is still the
case in Puerto Rico and other cane sugar-growing
countries.

The revolution changed this for Cuba. There was
still a "dead season," but at least there were ample jobs
to be found in other industries. As a consequence many
skilled sugar mill workers stayed on their new jobs, no
longer switching jobs and living places with the change
of seasons.

With the new stress on the importance of sugar production, and with the need to prepare for the 1970 harvest, a number of steps were undertaken that show
how serious the government is in its determination to
attain its sugar objectives. It has guaranteed a full

year's work to sugar mill workers, based on their highest rates of hourly pay. The aim is to bury the "dead season" once and for all. The government has made a strong plea to former, experienced sugar mill hands to return to their old jobs, wherever that is possible. Older workers, who have reached retirement age, have been asked to remain for the 1970 harvest and to impart their invaluable experience to the training of a younger generation of skilled mill workers.

These are not the measures of disorganized, scatterbrained people without a sense of planning. They are well planned deliberate steps to attain their goal, evincing a high degree of preparation. This does not negate all the criticisms made by the foreign efficiency expert quoted earlier. There is also much sloppy work and Cubans are the first to admit this.

Of course, all the above mentioned examples of concentrated effort may not be enough to guarantee the harvest. There is many a slip twixt planning and planting, planting and harvesting, harvesting and milling. If climatic conditions are poor, as much as 40 per cent of the crop can be ruined. Cuban leaders point to the draught conditions of the past two years for the poor showing and failure to meet goals.

A double-sized crop needs the doubling of just about everything right down the line. The acreage planted must be commensurably greater; so with the weeding, fertilizing, amount of fertilizer used, cane cutting, transport of cane stalks to the mills, and the milling itself. Any falling short, any breakdown at any point, can endanger the size and quality of the crop. And at each juncture these doubled tasks demand nearly doubled man-hours of work, for the process of mechanization has nowhere reached the point at which a sizeable reduction in hand labor is possible. This is particularly true in respect to cane-cutting.

As soon as the 1969 crop was cut, even before the cutting was over, the big push began for planting the 1970 crop. We saw signs of this in every province. Workers were being mustered as voluntary hands after work and on weekends, and in some cases were even taken off their regular jobs to help extend the planted acreage to that needed for a double crop. Each province and region had its own quota; before I left Cuba nearly every province had gone over the top.

One feature of the new planting also indicates more careful planning. Staggered so that the harvesting can be handled in batches and not all at one time, the first phase of the 1970 *zafra* has already begun in Camaguey province in September 1969, as this is being written, and will continue in spells for the rest of the year, with peak periods coming in the late fall and winter.

Some criticism has been leveled against the entire plan of doubling sugar production. Leo Huberman and Paul M. Sweezy, in their latest book on Cuba (*Socialism in Cuba,* New York, 1969), claim that this effort is a wasteful utilization of resources and energies. According to them, the same concentration of effort in other directions would be more economical and bring higher returns.

I am also aware that the Cuban leadership has altered its thinking on the significance of sugar production since the first years of the revolution. At first the emphasis was more on diversification of agriculture. The Cuban leaders now admit that the process of diversification was seen, mistakenly, as taking place at the expense of sugar production. In one speech delivered by Fidel in 1961, he even belittled the importance of sugar as a "cash crop," stressing instead the importance of cattle raising. The people of the world, he said, are not hungry for sugar; they are hungry for meat. Yet this very same leadership has now come to the conclusion that sugar cane is the most "natural" crop for Cuba; a crop most suited to her soil and climatic conditions, thereby most easily grown and enlarged.

I asked Cuban friends whether there was any guarantee of a market for ten million tons. I was told that this is the least of their worries. The Soviet Union and other socialist countries have agreed to take up to seven million tons. Cuba also has a quota of a couple million tons under the world sugar agreement. The Cubans have also learned, I was told, that sugar molasses can be used as fodder for cattle and is superior to corn in protein content. "We can use all the cane we harvest and more," they claim.

Under no circumstances is Cuba returning to a system of monoculture with sugar as its single, dominant marketable crop. It is to be the largest and most important *single* crop, but by no means dominant in the economy. The very increase in sugar production is seen as the way to earn greater foreign exchange with which to speed up the pace of diversification, mechanization and industrialization. Above all, the aim is most rapidly to overcome present shortages and rapidly raise the material and cultural well-being of the people.

Cuba has been compelled to borrow heavily to keep its head above water for a number of reasons. A bourgeois revolution puts a class in power that already possesses important means of production and the know-how to run them. A socialist revolution brings to power the class that labors but has no direct experience in ownership and operation of the economy. Every socialist revolution, particularly those in underdeveloped countries, faces the problem of leaning how to manage. Mistakes are inevitable and undoubtedly Cuba has made her share of them.

The revolution is called upon to do something immediate about the health and welfare of its people, even before the new economic system is able to make ends meet to cover these expenditures. Two such needs are universal free education and free medical services, both requiring immense sums for building physical facilities and even larger sums for operation. Already in 1965, the Cuban Government was spending an average of $19.15 per person per year for medical services. Mexico, ever so much larger, richer and more developed, with immense natural resources, spent in that same year only $1.98 for the health of each inhabitant—10 per cent of the amount spent by Socialist Cuba. Argentina came closest to Cuba in Latin America, spending $5.89 per person, only 30 per cent of the Cuban expenditure. Ecuador was at the bottom of the Latin American list, spending only 63 cents per capita for the medical needs of its people. The other Latin American countries were closer to the Ecuadorian average than to the Argentinian or Mexican ones.

The economic blockade imposed by the U.S. Government also has operated as a factor draining Cuban resources. Cuba has asked the Soviet Union, more than five thousand miles away, to supply her gasoline and fuel oil needs. Without this aid, Cuba's economy including all electric power, would have been paralyzed. The blockade has also meant a temporary crisis in obtaining U.S. machine parts. This has been met by buying these through intermediaries, by learning hov to duplicate them in Cuba, or by junking U. S. ma chines for newer models manufactured in other countries.

Enormous investments are needed to begin the long difficult climb from underdevelopment to modern development. Dams, factories, power stations, fertilizer plants, all cost vast sums that do not yield immediate returns.

These are some of the main reasons for Cuba's indebtedness and continuing trade deficit. In a recent interview with the world press, held in Lima, Peru in April, 1969, Carlos Rafael Rodríguez, one of the top leaders of Cuban Communist party and the government, who has intimate knowledge of Cuba's economy, listed some of the main Cuban creditors.

The largest is the Soviet Union which has given Cuba two long-term loans for economic development, totaling $230 million, as well as regular yearly commercial credits to make up for trade deficits. In 1968 alone the latter amounted to nearly $200 million. The interest on these loans and credits runs from two to 2.5 per cent a year. Cuba also has received $60 million in credits from the German Democratic Republic and $50 million from Rumania. Lesser amounts of credit have come from other socialist states. Sizeable credits have also come from Great Britain and France; the first for $50 million to build a huge fertilizer plant, and the latter, $36 million to purchase French tractors.

Cuba is anxious and determined to prove her ability to pay off her creditors, to end her yearly trade imbalances, and to lay a solid foundation upon which to get even larger amounts of long-term credits for an even faster pace of economic development. This is what "10 AN" means for the Cubans and why this is called the year of the decisive effort.

It is impossible to separate the shorter-range goal of ten million tons from the many longer-range plans already under way. As we have said previously, these are interdependent; they impinge on one another. Speaking with Carlos Rafael Rodríguez in the party headquarters in Havana after I had toured the island, I responded to his inquiry about my impressions by saying that I thought they would reach their goal of sugar production for 1970, barring some unforeseen disaster. But I did not see how they could continue to expend the same amount of man-hours for future crops and still have the labor available to continue and complete the many other projects under way throughout the island.

Old, pre-revolutionary Cuba had a vast army of unemployed, somewhere between 20 to 25 per cent of the labor force, depending on the season of the year. New Cuba has a grave labor shortage. I could easily use half a million to a million additional workers. The cutting of the sugar cane crops of recent years required a major mobilization of workers from the cities. Some even had to leave their regular jobs for weeks at a time to help bring the crop in. The 1970 crop will require the mustering of an urban labor force much larger than ever before and working at more frequent intervals and for longer periods of time.

Getting enlistments for this army of voluntary cane-cutters was well under way long before the crop itself had begun to sprout. In every city and hamlet, in every factory, office, school and institution, in every mass organization of the people, volunteers were being recruited for the coming harvest. Yet everywhere I went I found other plans and tasks in progress, each of which required an increasing expenditure of human labor. How then were all these to get done? Was there not the danger of a massive breakdown at some point along the way?

There are two main solutions to this problem: a more rapid tapping of woman-power reserves and the rapid mechanization of cane-cutting. The first of these was being worked on. In 1964, there were 282,000 women employed in production; in 1968, 371,000, or an increase of about 32%. In agriculture, however, there was no increase from 1964 to 1968, with only 55,000 to 60,000 women employed throughout this period.

To free women for employment will be a lengthy process involving many things, especially overcoming male prejudices against the employment of women. Many Cuban men are still conditioned by former mass unemployment and by traditional attitudes toward women. These attitudes stand in the way of using women's great but dormant abilities for the good of the whole people. It will also require a struggle in the minds of women themselves. This will take time. The country's manpower needs for the next years ahead will require more radical and immediate measures.

Rapid mechanization of cane-cutting is therefore a pressing necessity. But this cannot happen without finding the means to finance the construction or purchase of expensive mechanical cane-cutters in large quantities. The success of the 1970 harvest can give the country the leeway and flexibility with which to begin to solve the manpower crisis in the only way it can be solved — by getting more and more machines to take over the backbreaking work done today by hand.

Carlos Rafael said that the leadership is now working on the overall economic goals for the decade of the 1970s. He thinks the problem of mechanical cane-cutting will be solved in a few years. It is expected that the first 200 mechanical cane-cutters will be built in time for use in the 1970 harvest. Engineers have been work to eliminate certain mechanical bugs and to produce a machine that specifically meets local needs. It is believed this has now been accomplished. The plan also calls for 300 additional cane-cutting machines per year until a total of 1,500 are in use. At this point, it is believed, most cane-cutting will no longer be done by hand and only 100,000 of the very best *macheteros* will still be doing it the hard way.

These are the plans. Should new, unforeseen snags develop in this timetable, an even more acute manpower problem could arise.

5   Of Cattle, Oranges and Eternal Spring

The longer-range goals also have immediate requirements which demand a concentration of resources and energies. Sugar growing is not being expanded at the expense of diversification, nor is the great stress on agriculture leading to the neglect of certain important aspects of industrialization.

In 1959, for example, Cuba's merchant marine consisted of only 14 ships with a total capacity of 57,974 tons; in 1969, there were 49 ships with a total capacity of 376,680 tons. In 1959, Cuba produced some 1,700 million kilowatt hours of electricity; in 1971 it will surpass 3,700 million kilowatt hours. At the beginning of the revolution Cuba produced 850,000 tons of cement per year; it is now approaching two million tons and by 1971 is expected to produce 2.2 million tons a year.

In Cienfuegos we visited the construction site of a huge fertilizer plant which, when in full operation in 1971, will produce 465,000 tons of chemical fertilizer. The construction plan is British, with British engineers guiding the work. The labor force is mainly composed of youth who are part of a nationally formed Communist Construction Brigade. When we were there construction was 40 days ahead of schedule. This plant is costing Cuba $40 million for construction and $60 million more for installation. When completed it will produce from one-fourth to one-third of all the fertilizer needs of the country, saving about $80 a ton in foreign exchange.

Agricultural diversification is moving along quickly. A few years ago Cuba reduced her rice acreage because she found it cheaper to buy rice abroad. Not now. Huge acreages have been turned over to the growing of a new strain of rice, sturdier, easier to plant, and with a much larger yield. In the province of Pinar del Rio alone, 50,000 acres of rice have been planted this year. Fidel Castro has promised that in the very year that it produces ten million tons of sugar, Cuba will also harvest a bonanza crop of 150,000 to 200,000 tons of rice. In 1971 she expects to have a large rice surplus for export.

There have also been vast increases in the planting of coffee, cotton, tobacco, pineapples, bananas and citrus fruits. In the 70 years of U.S. exploitation of Cuban natural resources, the forest areas of the country were denuded in the interests of larger and larger U.S.-owned sugar plantations. During the first seven years of the revolution nearly 300 million fruit and lumber trees were planted. Tree planting continues; I was told that by 1974, Cuba expects to grow more oranges than any country in the world.

Around the city of Havana a broad belt of green, *El Cordón,* has been grown. Coffee plants, citrus fruits and other crops run for mile upon mile. The green belt is manned by the people of the city and aims to make Havana self-sufficient in food. Similar cordons have been erected around other cities as well.

Before the revolution Cuba, like Puerto Rico today, had one of the highest food import rates in the world. This is understandable for a country whose soil and climate are not suitable for agriculture. But Cuba is a lush, fertile island, capable of feeding her population many times over. Only the plunder of her soil in the interests of large foreign and native landholders, and the profits of U.S. food exporters explain this criminal state of affairs. Cuba's soil is being used today in a planned way, first to feed the Cuban people and then to earn the means with which to win the total war against underdevelopment.

A revolution is literally taking place in animal live-stock breeding and especially in cattle-raising. We saw more henneries and more chicks being transported on huge vans to new homes than we thought existed in all the world. Egg production increases steadily and has already reached more than 100 million eggs a month. The great stress on cattle raising has one immediate objective: to overcome most rapidly all shortages in milk and dairy products so that this vital protein food is available in ample quantities for children *and* adults as well. A second important objective is to greatly increase the total meat supply of the country. When these two aims are achieved, Cuba will be in a position to consider exporting her surplus dairy and meat products.

The problem of cattle-raising was under animated discussion wherever we went. In Santiago de Cuba we were cornered by a young man who proceeded to give us a lecture on the technical aspects of scientific cattle-raising, including his opinion of the policy differences in this field. He was so knowledgeable and had such strong views on the subject that I was convinced he was a *técnico*, an expert, in this work. But no, he was just following the debate in the press and participating in it too.

The debate centers on the traditional Cuban cow, the Cebú, a hardy animal capable of withstanding the long dry season of December to May, when other less sturdy breeds of cattle would waste away and die from lack of water and grass. Even the Cebú tends to fatten during the seven months of water and to lose weight rapidly during the five dry ones. But while the Cebú can survive under these conditions, it is an extremely poor milker, giving on an average only two to two and one-half liters of milk a day. Therefore it cannot meet the dairy needs of the people.

Consequently a vast project is under way to create a new breed of cattle capable of withstanding Cuba's dry season and of meeting her dairy needs. This is being done by mating the Cebú with the Holstein, a good milker. All over the country stations for artificial insemination have been established and by the spring of 1968, some 500,000 offspring of this "marriage" were the first members of a new breed called the F-1.

The F-1 cow, it is claimed, combines the hardiness of the Cebú with the milk-giving qualities of the Holstein. Official statistics claim that this new breed gives an average of ten liters of milk a day, or about four times the Cebú average. A second generation of this genetic process, the F-2, reportedly gives as much as 20 liters a day. Some two million cows were in the insemination program and on the basis of the first results the expectation was that by 1971-72 the shortage of dairy products would give way to surplus.

What then is there to debate? It would seem that the answer has been found, but some disagree. At the recent Congress of the Institute of Animal Science, three British scientists presented a paper and delivered speeches challenging the official statistics and claiming that the F-1 cow was not what she was said to be. They also opposed the idea of using sugarcane molasses as feed, insisting that corn was the best fodder.

Fidel himself became involved in this debate. He delivered a speech to the closing session of the congress analyzing in detail every criticism made and rejecting many of them. At the same time he said that the Institute had not and would not ban independent research work. "We will never adopt a dogmatic position; the Revolution will always listen to the truth, to the results, to the facts about research work," Castro promised. "It will always listen to any positive ideas; it will never be dogmatic in this field. If someday, in opposition to the Revolution's point of view, it should be proved unequivocably that corn is the solution — something we do not believe will happen — there will be no political obstacles — that is a thing of the past in our country — there will be no social obstacles, there will be no stubborness, there will be no dogmatism; corn will be accepted."

It is interesting to note that this entire debate, including the paper and speeches of the British scientists, was printed in the pages of *Granma*. That is how a

Controversy and hope surround this F-1 cow and her newborn, F-2 offspring.

young man in Santiago de Cuba knew so much about the subject and why the whole people could form their own opinions.

Artificial insemination is being used on an extensive scale not only with cattle, but in all forms of animal husbandry—hogs, chickens, and even, according to an article in *Granma*, in the fertilizing of fish eggs. While the press was discussing the virtues of the F-1 cow, especially during the sessions of the Institute, the daily newspaper of the youth, *El Juventud Rebelde* (Rebel Youth), carried a piece in its weekend humor supplement, *DDT*.

It described a session between a bull and a psychiatrist. The bull complains about emotional problems and asks the doctor for help. He tells him that he comes from a good, stable family, had a happy childhood, loved his father, never got hit on the head, yet now has problems. The trouble is, he confides, that he works for an insemination center and never had contact with cows. Once every four days he is led into a stall alongside other bulls in similar stalls, awaiting the mechanical job of semen extraction. The very sight of the other animals, the color of their hides, their smell, arouses him and he imagines himself mounting an animal. And then, suddenly, the spell is broken, it is all over, he has been tricked again. The psychiatrist tells him the cause of his neurosis is clear—it is a lack of contact with cows. But, continues the good doctor, you have a job to do, your duty to the revolution must come first, you must forget about cows, you must just drive them from your mind. But, doctor, protests the patient, that is exactly why I'm here. My problem is that I've forgotten about cows. Now I dream of bulls.

The main aspect of the longer-range agricultural program is depicted in Cuba as the "Struggle for Eternal Spring." We have said that Cuba has an extremely fertile soil and a wonderful growing climate. The story of Jack and the Beanstalk could have been written of Cuba or Puerto Rico, for in either country one can virtually throw a seed out the window one day, and see a plant flowering there the next day.

Cuba could have three crops a year almost everywhere, except for one thing — water. Cuba has an average, or even an above average, yearly rainfall. But averages mean nothing if all the rain falls in one part of the year and none in the other. And it is especially meaningless where there are no snowcapped mountains, great lakes or large rivers capable of holding water for any period of time.

In temperate climates there is a blanket of snow on the ground during the winter which melts in the spring and nourishes the meadowland. But in Cuba there is no snow, and when the rains come they come in torrents, saturate the earth, even devastate regions by causing immense floods, and then get swallowed by the soil and run off in underground and surface streams to the sea. As mentioned earlier, the destruction of Cuba's forests by imperialist exploiters also robbed the land of another means to hold water.

Only where the land is below sea level is water stored for a time, but in stagnant, mosquito-infested swamplands, unfit for human habitation or agriculture. How to conserve water, how to save it for the dry season, is Cuba's big problem.

The struggle for eternal spring is a struggle for water. It is a task which requires the building of dams, reservoirs and drainage systems, linking them all together in a criss-cross network of irrigation canals that nourish the earth with life-giving water. This great undertaking is also under way.

We visited the great new dam at Contramaestre in Oriente province. Its capacity is 198 million cubic meters of water. In 1958, the total reservoir capacity in all of pre-revolutionary Cuba was less than 30 million cubic meters of water; in 1968, more than one billion cubic meters. In the province of Pinar del Rio, to the west of Havana, 125 dams and reservoirs are under construction. The same is true all over the country.

Fidel Castro has said that within a period of no more than five years, the vast majority of Cuba's tillable lands will be irrigated. In his address to the Institute of Animal Science, Fidel told the meeting of scientists, technicians and farm workers that, "10,000 machines are at work in this country building roads, canals, dams and irrigation systems and drilling wells for the solution of one of the greatest natural difficulties found in this country: cyclical draughts. There are 10,000 machines and over 60,000 men operating those machines working on all these projects."

Proof of what can be done is to be seen in Southern California. This area was once a barren desert; today it is one of the most fertile regions in the world. Cuba's soil and climate are vastly superior. When every season is springtime in Cuba, it will be the most beautiful garden in the world.

6 Revolution Cuban Style

Cuban music has a beat distinctly its own, as does its style of revolution. Every revolution is somewhat different from those that preceded it and contributes something new to world revolutionary experience. This is surely true of the Cuban Revolution. It took place under considerably different and unique circumstances. When to these are added Cuba's particular temperament and psychology arising out of her whole historic background, and the special conditions in which her ongoing revolution continues to develop, the result is a Marxist-Leninist tune played with a rumba-like rhythm.

The socialist revolutions preceding the Cuban came consequent to two great world war crises. The Eastern European and Asian revolutions following World War II took place back to back, so to speak. Their rear was protected by the existence and sustained with the aid of the Soviet Union. Most of the East European revolutions were protected from within as well by the presence of the Soviet Army after its rout of the Nazi legions.

The Cuban Revolution was different. It, too, has been sustained by Soviet material aid and by the support of socialist, national liberation and peace forces throughout the world. But it did not burst forth under conditions of external, inter-imperialist war, but rather through internal guerrilla war. Cuba's borders are not flanked by socialist states; it is geographically isolated from them. It lives in a hostile sea of bristling U.S. armament; Guantanamo Bay is still occupied by the

Pentagon, and the colossus itself is just across the Florida straits.

Cuba is not a country of tens of millions of people. It has but eight million, more or less the same as New York City. It is a small island of only 44,000 square miles as compared with the 3.5 million square miles of the United States. And its socialist revolution triumphed in a country where few people believed it possible, prior to a socialist revolution in the United States itself.

These factors have left their mark on Cuban thinking. They have produced the special Cuban style. Having won against the mature opinion of some who were sure it could not be done that way, it is quite understandable why Cuban leadership tends to be irreverent toward set opinions of what is and what is not possible.

As a small island people, the Cubans have always had to fight for their freedom against what appeared to be insuperable odds. This was true of the war against Spain and the struggle against Yankee domination. It was true of the *Granma* landing and the guerrilla war. It is true of the efforts to defeat the blockade and in the magnitude of the campaign to overcome underdevelopment. It is no wonder then that the Cuban Revolution places such stress on the decisive role of consciousness and the moral readiness to sacrifice as expressed in their slogan, *Patria o Muerte* — Country or Death.

Without this moral quality the assault on the Moncada Barracks would never have been undertaken, nor the landing of *Granma*, nor the determination to carry on when only 12 of the original band remained. Without a total disregard for past precedents and so-called "odds" they never would have had the courage and foresight to develop the democratic anti-imperialist revolution into a socialist one. And without the same kind of conviction and moral fiber there would not have been the firmness displayed at the time of the Bay of Pigs invasion and the October 1962 missile crisis, nor what is demonstrated today in the fight for national development.

These are some of the elements that have helped produce a close, even intimate, relationship between the leaders and the people in Cuba; a constant stress on the decisive role of human will and consciousness; and a certain revolutionary puritanism sprinkled at times with touches of romanticism, yet devoid of schematic sectarian dogmatism.

I asked the industrial efficiency man mentioned previously, who had been so critical of everything Cuban, whether the revolution still enjoyed the same popularity it had at the outset. He answered without hesitation: "There can be no doubt of it; 90 per cent of the Cubans are for the revolution and for Fidel."

"It would therefore seem to me," I said, "that the Cubans *do* know how to do some things rather well. They successfully led the first socialist revolution in the hemisphere and, now, after ten years of immense difficulties and some mistakes they still have the people enthusiastically with them. How do you explain this?"

"Well," he replied, "Fidel is so typically Cuban. He knows the people and they find their reflection in him. They are so much alike."

This is an oversimplification of the matter, of course. The mass support for the revolution springs from a deeper fount than the ability of the people to identify with one man, or he with them. It comes from the profound belief that the revolution is truly theirs. No matter what mistakes may have been made or may still be made, the revolution belongs to them and its future is their future. Yet there is a certain element of truth in what he said. The people do identify most closely with Fidel. He has become the living personification of the revolution as Che Guevara has become its martyred saint. And, if the people have such confidence in the revolution and its *lider máximo,* Castro's style of leadership has much to do with this.

There have been jests about Fidel's relish for long-winded speeches. Not until I visited Cuba and heard Castro speak did I understand why the people listened to him so intently, often traveling for many miles and standing for long hours to do so. Fidel is not a demagogic "rabble-rouser." He does not indulge in revolutionary rhetoric or play to his audience for applause. He is less the agitator and more the propagandist and educator. He discusses with the people the most important and complex questions, as if talking to each of them separately. His aim is to elevate their comprehension, not to talk down to them. He takes them into his confidence and explains, explains, explains, with an intimacy and sincerity that make people hang on his every word.

I heard Fidel speak three times while in Cuba; twice over radio and once in person. The first speech was delivered to the Congress of Animal Science previously referred to. Here he debated those critical of policies in this field. He even mentioned that some of his critics had nicknamed him "the Prime Minister of Genetics." He admitted his lack of scientific training and expressed his desire to learn from those who knew more.

Che Guevara is honored in the Town Square of Holguín,
Oriente province.

At the same time he vigorously defended the duty of the leadership to make final decisions, especially where there was divided counsel as to how and where the limited resources of the nation were to be invested. He also defended the right and the duty of a prime minister to be deeply concerned with the problem of providing more milk and meat for the people. This speech was broadcast throughout the island.

A week later Castro spoke at a conference of *técnicos*. He was quite critical, at points even negative, in his appraisal of how some things were going. The country, he said, was still moving forward with only a fraction of its potential power. He criticized administrative bodies that go their own way and make no attempt to coordinate overlapping efforts with other agencies. He warned that the 1970 harvest was by no means in the bag, that bad weather could damage it, and called for measures that would guarantee ten million tons, rain or no rain. This speech too was broadcast.

Then I heard him speak in person at a great outdoor, after-work demonstration of hundreds of thousands of people in the Plaza of the Revolution. The occasion was the visit of Tran Buu Kiem, representative of the National Liberation Front of South Vietnam. For days the country had been preparing to give its guest a great people's welcome. Castro spoke for about one and one-half hours. He explained the history of the war of aggression against Vietnam and the objectives of U.S. imperialism. He analyzed the NLF ten-point peace program and explained why it was a logical foundation for a just peace. He then compared it with the eight-point program of Nixon and why the Nixon plan was a sham, could never bring peace and was not intended to do so. With passion and eloquence he spoke of what

Vietnam meant to Cuba and how its heroism had also defended Cuba from invasion. He repeated the pledge to give the Vietnamese whatever they asked for, including readiness to shed Cuban blood itself. He analyzed the contradictions besetting U.S. imperialism and paid high tribute to the anti-war struggle and sentiment of the North American people.

Castro is not the only Cuban leader who discusses national and world questions before the entire people, but his voice is the most authoritative and gets the widest hearing. Through the use of great mass rallies, and especially by means of radio and television, the leadership has done a great deal to develop mass consciousness and mass confidence in plans and policies. Shortcomings and mistakes are not hidden. They are explained.

Another aspect of Fidel's style that has caught on with the rest of the leadership is the spending of a great deal of time in the interior of the country, meeting with people, discussing problems as they arise. By now, hardly a Cuban has not seen Fidel in the flesh at least once, and there is many a Cuban who has cornered him in some factory, field or cattle insemination station, to lodge a criticism, ask a question, or make a suggestion.

It is extremely difficult to find the leaders in their offices in Havana. Appointments to see them depend upon when they return to Havana and how long they might be there. Each leading person has his own specific economic battlefront in addition to his other tasks. This makes for a certain amount of chaos. It is defended as guaranteeing the most important thing at this time – close ties with the people at the fronts where the breakthroughs have to be made.

Employees in the administrative agencies in Havana, no matter how important their responsibilities, are asked to volunteer their labor for manual agricultural tasks. This is part of a campaign to "enhance proletarian awareness" and to "increase revolutionary consciousness" in the administrative apparatus. Raul Castro, in a speech delivered on May 1, 1968, in Camaguey, referred to this as part of a campaign "against bureaucracy." He said that the "herulean tasks of the Havana Green Belt have provided a revolutionary stimulus of great importance for the capital, especially to our administrative agencies and services." According to him, "Not only the physical appearance of the outskirts of Havana, but also the character and administrative procedure of our central agencies, have been transformed in this process." It is hard to say how much of this is the human quirk of turning necessity into virtue. For, if we understand Raul correctly, he is saying that this use of administrative personnel for volunteer agricultural labor has not hurt administrative work, but has helped it.

Administrative workers are also taken from their desks four to six weeks at a time for cane-cutting. People I talked with defended this practice on still broader grounds. They said it prevents a separation between physical and mental labor, between administrative and productive work, between city and countryside. It makes office personnel more respectful of those who produce by the sweat of their brows and prevents the rural population from becoming estranged from the people in the cities.

Actually this emphasis flows also from how Fidel and the other leaders view their own roles. They do not see themselves as technical administrators of a centralized economy, but as leaders of the people in a vast, continuous, many-sided war against backwardness and for the knowledge, culture and morality that is needed for a communist society.

7 Moral and Material Incentives

The Cubans combine the use of moral and material incentives in a variety of patterns, depending upon the given situation and need. To a certain degree this can be said of all socialist countries. But while Cuba employs both methods, or rather a combination of both, it tends to view material incentives as an undesirable but unavoidable necessity and moral incentives as a preference to be used and emphasized at all times.

I believe it is wrong to make an artificial separation between moral and material incentives. The greatest material incentive of all is the knowledge that a new kind of society is being built and that as one contributes his utmost to the common effort the material and cultural needs of all the people will be fulfilled more swiftly. This is why people make revolutions. They desire to change a situation in which the wealth they produce is stolen from them. They wish to build a society in which social wealth can be multiplied greatly for the benefit of all the people.

Moral incentives are therefore also material incentives. The Cubans know this. They constantly explain what an end to underdevelopment will mean in concrete, material, human terms. But the difference lies in their approach to *individual* material incentives.

The Cubans prefer that the material benefits attained by the people be *mass* as against individual in character. Many such mass material incentives, or benefits, have been won already and many more are on their way. Public telephone serivce, for example, is now free; just pick up a public phone and dial. Athletic events are free, and Cubans are wild *aficianados* of *beisbol* and sports. Public education is free from nursery through university, including textbooks, paper, notebooks and pencils. State-supported scholarship students and boarding school students get food, clothing and shelter free. No one pays more than 10 per cent of their income for rent and after 1970 all housing is to be rent-free. Already about 10 per cent of Cuban families, those who have lived in the same dwellings for many years, no longer pay rent. Medical and hospital care is free, and all funeral expenses are met by the government. A social security law guaranteeing old age pensions has just been adopted.

The magnitude of these material benefits can only be appreciated when it is remembered that Cuba is still a poor, underdeveloped country. For the sake of more rapid economic growth, 30 per cent of Cuba's gross national product was plowed back into the economy in 1968. This amounted to $1.24 billion — not a tremendously large investment sum for the United States, but it is quite a chunk for Cuba.

Cubans argue in favor of mass as against individual incentives, and stress the moral incentive as key, in this way: We recognize that we are a long way from a full communist society. We still have quite a way to go even to become a developed socialist society. But we believe we must build socialism and communism simultaneously. If we draw too hard and fast a line between these two stages we may find ourselves in deep trouble in years to come.

The José Martí Housing Project

This stress is somewhat different from that found in classical Marxist writings. Marx, Engels and Lenin placed great emphasis on the distinctions between what they called the "first phase" and the "higher phase" of the new society. In the first phase, which would last a rather lengthy period of time, each worker would receive a "corresponding quantity of products" to the amount of work performed. Lenin wrote that during this first phase each worker would receive from society "as much as he has given it" (*State and Revolution*). Marx foresaw that the higher phase of the new collective society would be one in which each person contributed according to his abilities and received from the storehouse of society according to his needs. But he pointed out that this higher communist stage of development could come only after the sharp distinction between physical and mental labor had disappeared, when labor itself had become more than a means to live but "life's prime necessity," and when "all the springs of cooperative wealth flow more abundantly" (*Critique of the Gotha Program*).

One Cuban argued his point of view with the following example. "Look," he said, "with the kind of climate we have and the relative ease with which we can meet housing and clothing needs as compared with countries with a colder climate, and with the revolution we are making in agriculture, it should be possible for us in about 25 years actually to give every person all the material things he needs. But if at that time people still think in the selfish terms of personal gain, in egotistical ways, if they still think about money, then we will be no closer to a communist society. If we want a communist society it is not enough to establish the economic base for it, it is necessary to change the way men think to win them ideologically for a new kind of society."

Raul Castro summed this up in the following words: "A spirit of work gives rise to a greater spirit of work; awareness engenders more awareness; valor and faith engender greater valor and faith; honest attitudes engender more honest attitudes; love of society, of all the people and of humanity engenders greater love among men. But if we think in terms of selfishness; ambition will engender more ambition; opportunism, more opportunism; corruption, more corruption; rampant individualism, more individualism. And, for that reason, we refuse to erect an altar to the god Money and to prostrate man's conscience at his feet."

How does this work in practice? We have said that the Cubans have a preference but are flexible in their approach. In the city of Holguín, Oriente province, we visited the new Lenin Hospital. The Soviet Union had made a gift of this hospital with equipment for 450 beds. The Cubans increased its capacity to 900 beds. Before the revolution this region of some 400,000 human beings had only five small hospitals and no polyclinics. Now there are 26 hospitals and 29 polyclinics. In 1958, only 40,000 pesos were spent on hospitals in this region; in 1968, 10 million pesos.

Socialized medicine, the construction of hospitals, the spread of medical services into the rural areas, increased the need for doctors astronomically. More than half of Cuba's MD's were located in Havana before the revolution. With the advent of the revolution many doctors fled the country for the United States. To meet this crisis the government agreed to pay doctors 600 pesos a month, much more than the average wage or salary, yet considerably less than the 3,000 to

The new Lenin Hospital in the city of Holquín, Oriente province, a gift of the Soviet Union.

4,000 pesos earned monthly by physicians before the revolution. The government also permitted doctors who wished to maintain a private practice to continue doing so after their hours in public health.

This is still the arrangement, but the most recent graduating classes of the three medical universities in Cuba started something new. The graduates took a voluntary oath that they would never engage in private practice as long as they lived. They also agreed to forego accepting the 600 pesos salary and to start with about half that amount. The purpose was to bring doctors' salaries more in line with those in other occupations and to remove from physicians the stigma of serving the people for the sake of money. These young doctors also agreed to accept posts in rural communities for a minimum of two years following graduation.

One of the older gray-headed doctor administrators at the Lenin Hospital described this change to us. He was still getting the 600 pesos a month he was entitled to, although from his responsibilities and approach I gathered he had given up private practice. When he talked to us about these young doctors, their dedication, their determination to make the Hippocratic Oath mean something once again, his eyes glistened and his voice bespoke great admiration and even envy. He said to us: "We now have more doctors than we had before the revolution and believe me they are better doctors: first, because of their love of humanity; and second, because medicine now serves all the people and not just a few well-to-do, and our doctors therefore get far more experience in treating every kind of illness than was ever possible before."

This spirit is spreading. What the young doctors are doing is not an exception. University professors were getting 750 pesos a month; the new ones now take 300 to 350 pesos a month. Teachers used to work one shift in one school and then take another shift elsewhere and receive double pay. This is not against the law, but an ideological campaign has been conducted to convince teachers that after their basic earnings additional work should be voluntary, that otherwise they demean themselves by seeing money as life's chief objective. The same is true of other intellectuals. They could undertake a number of separate tasks, such as lecturing, writing, etc., and get paid for each. Now the emphasis is on convincing them to accept a basic salary and to donate of their other time, and of their creativity, voluntarily.

Tipping in restaurants and hotels has also been eliminated. The workers in each place were called together to discuss this problem. It was admitted that many of them depend upon tips to make ends meet. They were asked whether they would agree to forego tips if their basic wage were increased to take what they made in tips into account. In one place after another the workers agreed and committees were set up to work out the practical arrangements. In all the different restaurants and hotels we visited we did not see a single tip offered or taken. When I tried to test this by leaving coins on the table, I was called back because I had "forgotten something." Honorariums may get slipped under the table here and there for some special favors, but I am convinced that there is a public onus against it which seems to have the support of most waiters and other service employees.

On the north coast of Oriente, some 39 kilometers from Holguín, we visited the small town of Gíbara. Once a terribly depressed area, earnings here used to average about 40 centavos a week. When Che Guevara first visited the region he was aghast at what he saw and urged that something be done immediately. It was decided to build a textile mill and to organize a fishing cooperative; both exist today and are doing exceedingly well.

The textile mill was built according to Japanese specifications and was installed with Japanese machinery. Japanese engineers also helped guide the construction and taught the workers how to operate the machinery. This modern, air-conditioned plant employing 272 workers is named after a Japanese socialist leader, Inejiro Asanuma, who was murdered while participating in a popular demonstration in Japan while the plant was being built.

After visiting all parts of the plant, including the laboratory and machine shop, manned exclusively by local residents, we spent about an hour in the office of the plant manager discussing various aspects of the plant's operation. In addition to the manager, five or six workers crowded into the office with us. After learning that the average wage of the workers was six pesos a day for a six day week, I asked the manager whether I could ask him a personal question. I wanted to know what his salary was.

He began by giving us a lecture. He was a revolutionist and not working for money. The greatest honor in his life was that he was chosen to manage this first industrial enterprise in the community. What greater reward could he ask? I started to fidget and feel ashamed at having asked the question. Then I became somewhat suspicious that he was trying to dodge a direct answer. But finally he said, "You have asked the question, so I will tell you. My salary is 142 pesos a month." Then with a slight flourish of the hand he pointed to one of the workers standing near the door. "That comrade," he said, "is the plant sweeper. He earns 138 pesos a month. Now you know why the workers can discuss all their problems with me, domestic ones too, for we are all one, live in the same community and lead the same kind of lives."

Yet in other places I visited I found men getting considerably above the average wage. The rule seems to be flexible. Where higher pay, or extra pay, is necessary to get people to make a greater effort, and where particular skill is essential, it is paid. An example is the inducement offered sugar mill workers to keep them on the job all year long and to persuade those who left to return. Each worker is guaranteed a full year's work at his premium hourly rate of pay.

At the same time the ideological struggle aims at convincing more and more workers to contribute their maximum efforts for moral-ideological reasons and not for extra remuneration. How much success this campaign is having can be seen by the fact that by May 1968, 121,134 workers, or approximately 10 per cent of the organized work force of Cuba, had voluntarily given up their overtime pay for extra hours of work.

There are some who question whether this stress on overtime work is the most effective long range method to increase production. No doubt a percentage of those who contribute extra hours of labor without extra pay—maybe a majority now—do so as a consequence of social pressure and not out of total conviction. Furthermore, some workers, especially those with large families but only one breadwinner, actually need the extra money but feel ashamed to ask for it. Also I was told that during these extra hours of labor, discipline is more lax and that among voluntary cane-cutters considerable time is wasted.

Moreover, the weight of this extra voluntary labor falls heaviest on the backs of the most ideologically conscious workers who often contribute their weekends and vacations to push the work forward. We visited factories in which some workers had pledged to contribute as much as 1,000 extra hours of labor for the year. This averages out to about 20 extra hours of work per week. How long can such a physical strain be absorbed? There has been a recent increase in accidents at the sugar mills, and experience has shown that the rate of accidents increases each additional hour of work. Also, there may be a danger that the most advanced and most conscious workers will become physically and mentally exhausted and thus find it more difficult to play the steady, exemplary and leading role that they must.

Experience in advanced industrial countries shows that longer hours of work do not always lead to greater production results. Sometimes a shorter workday or week, with workers that are fresher and more rested, can accomplish more. Cuban workers do not work with the same intensity as do workers in the United States, from what we saw. Yet the more advanced workers, the ones who must carry the heaviest burden of contributing extra hours of labor, are precisely those wanting to increase labor productivity.

Armando Hart, Organizational Secretary of the party, deplores the high rate of absenteeism and the poor, inefficient organization of the workday. He says that this requires individual attention to each worker and his problems, better administration in each plant by steadily supplying raw materials and machine parts, and efficient and comprehensive coordination.

The Minister of Labor, Captain Jorge Risquit, has also pointed recently to the need for greater attention to what he calls the "rear guard": "A vanguard with communist conscientiousness regarding work is developing, but there still remains a 'rear guard' characterized by absenteeism, negligence and inadequate use of the workday."

The extreme pressure being exerted today for additional hours of labor, whether paid or not, arises from an emergency situation and the determination to reach the goals set for the year. In similar emergency situations there were great pressures for voluntary labor in the early years of the other socialist countries as well. It may be true, as many Cubans believe, that some socialist countries have now gone to an opposite extreme of stressing material above moral incentives. But one thing seems clear, at least to me—the present extreme pressure for increased hours of labor cannot be continued indefinitely. The only real answer is to increase overall productivity and efficiency, to more rapidly tap the reserves of woman power, and to speed up the process of mechanization which in turn requires more rapid training of a young generation knowledgeable in the ways of machinery and modern technology.

The great emphasis on overtime work without added remuneration has an important economic argument in its favor. With the existing shortages in consumer goods, any great increase in wages and salaries would exert an inflationary pressure, encouraging speculation and black-marketeering. But the Cubans I spoke with would challenge the view that this was a major consideration. One Cuban clinched his arguments in favor or moral incennntives in these words:

"In a capitalist country such as the United States,

there are people who work to build a revolutionary movement and a vanguard party. The people who join this movement are expected to be self-sacrificing, devoted fighters for the revolutionary cause. They are expected to give nearly all their free time, after work and weekends, for the party and the movement. They are expected to make sacrifices, whether prison or life itself, for their cause and for the people. Why should this change after the revolution? Why should we not build on the same high moral premise that not all people are selfish, and that people can work together for the common good and make sacrifices for it? Sure, we know that only a minority is ready to do this at first. But it should be our objective to convince everyone, and especially the rising generation, of the correctness of this view. When the whole people learn to think in this cooperative, unselfish way, when each finds his own personal fulfillment in work for the common good, then indeed will we have prepared well for communist society."

What is known in Cuba as the great "revolutionary offensive" to win the people against "economism" and "selfishness" was launched by Fidel Castro in March 1968. It was then that the big push for voluntary work began in earnest. In a few weeks time, 250,000 volunteers were enlisted for two, three or four weeks of intensive cane-cutting, cultivating, fertilizing or harvesting of coffee, fruit and other crops.

It was then too that the ideological campaign began to win people to give up extra pay for extra work, to accept reduction in salaries where these were too far above the general average, to stop accepting tips, and to place moral-ideological commitments above all others.

The revolutionary offensive also began the process of nationalizing the remaining private businesses, most of which were in the service trades. In two weeks time, 57,600 small businesses were nationalized and turned over to *El Poder Local*, the local government body in each region or municipality.

I wondered about the wisdom of taking over the small cockroach businesses at a time when the country had its hands full with the main economic tasks before it. I was told that it was precisely to help this greater effort that the nationalization was necessary. It appears that unscrupulous, selfish individuals were taking advantage of the shortage of consumer goods to enrich themselves. This was a bad example. It could be a demoralizing influence. Honest, hardworking people could say, "See how some *cabrones*, scoundrels, are permitted to feather their own nests at our expense." Furthermore, we were told, these private businesses were breeding parasitism and counter-revolution.

There is still another reason for the nationalization. At a time of acute labor shortage there is a feeling that it is uneconomical to have a considerable number of people waste their time and efforts on small pushcart-type businesses. Yet many of these small service enterprises did fill a certain need that the overall planned economy has not yet been able to meet. It is to be hoped that this gobbling up of all remaining private businesses at one swallow will prove to be a wise move, and that what was gained far outweighs what was lost.

All Cuban policies seem to be a blend between ideological and practical considerations. The approach to the small farmer is a good illustration of this. About 34 per cent of Cuba's tillable soil is still in private hands, divided into family-sized farms of no more than 165 acres each. When I asked whether the nationalization of small businesses presaged a future takeover of private farms, the answer was, "No, no, never!"

The small farmer, I was reminded, has been the staunch ally of the revolution. This will never be forgotten. Furthermore, the government had promised the small farmer that there will never be another agrarian reform, and never any kind of confiscation. And the Cuban revolution keeps its word. As the new society develops, Cubans argue, as the farmer realizes that he has much more to gain by collective effort, he will voluntarily relinquish his plot of land. But this will never be forced on him. Never, they emphasize.

Whether the process will be as simple as this only time will tell. What is clear at this point is that given two different kinds of private ownership — private business and private farming — and two different attitudes toward the revolution, two quite different policy approaches have emerged. Yet these approaches, seemingly contradictory, both flow from the same overall consideration — the strengthening of the revolution. Of course, policies and policy applications do get altered with changes in times and circumstances. Present emphases cannot be viewed as eternal verities. But it seems to me that some aspects of the Cuban style of revolution are of more than transient significance.

8   Cuba's Vanguard

History has many examples of spontaneous rebellion, few of successful social revolution. The reason is clear: a social revolution, as distinct from forced concessions or a mere change in palace guard, is the act by which one class is removed from power and replaced by another. The upper class in power has immense advantages. On its side are the administrative and repressive arms of government, the law and tradition. It has the invaluable experience of being a governing class and the arrogance and self-confidence to believe this is its god-given right. It has a large entourage of intellectual lackeys and administrative bureaucrats, from writers to court jesters, from judges to police sergeants, always ready to prostitute the truth in its defense.

To succeed, a social revolution must have popular support. This is essential, but in itself insufficient for victory. A spontaneous, popular upheaval can shake, even topple, a government. However, without conscious leadership, without a clear objective and strategy, the economic and political power that stands behind the old government cannot be demolished and replaced with a new economic and political power.

Thus the second ingredient for victory must be the existence of a tightly organized, highly disciplined, and ideologically clear leadership; in other words, a revolutionary vanguard. Without such a vanguard the revolution must flounder, its objectives remain confused, and its main strength — popular support — soon become dissipated and dispersed through internal strife and division.

When the Cuban *guerrilleros* marched down Havana's Fifth Avenue in their grimy, sweat-soaked olive-green uniforms, many people, including some in the U.S. State Department, expected a change in the form of governmental rule, but not in the class character of that rule. Some even had the illusion that all the State Department had to do to set things right with revolutionary Cuba was piously to wash its hands of the blood spilled by Batista. They soon learned to what degree they had misjudged the character of the revolution and the quality of its leadership.

The July 26th Movement led by Fidel Castro was not a political party in the formal sense. Yet the two years of guerrilla war had welded it into a tightly knit force. Its program represented the interests of the amalgam of democratic forces united around it. In broad outlines this called for the armed overthrow of the dictatorship and a return to constitutional government. But it did not stop there. It sought to tear up by the roots the social conditions that had brought the Batista dictatorship into being; namely, the oppression of the great majority of the Cuban people in the interests of U.S. corporations. It therefore pledged itself to basic revolutionary reforms — land to the peasants; a living wage for the workers; universal free education; an end to monoculture; and whatever steps were needed, including that of outright nationalization, to put an end to every form of U.S. imperialist domination.

It was the advanced program of an anti-imperialist, agrarian, and bourgeois democratic revolution. Behind it stood varied class and social forces and even different class ideologies.

The student youth that started the guerrilla war were mainly from the middle class, with a handful even from the upper class. These young people were motivated by a deep, all-consuming love of country and people and an intense hatred for the semi-colonial status of Cuba and the U.S.-dominated puppet dictatorship. They were animated with the fierce determination to complete the war for Cuban independence begun a century before by the two greatest Cuban heroes, José Martí and Antonio Maceo.

Some of these youth were led to the writings of Marx and Lenin in their search for answers to a world divided between a few rich nations and many poor ones, and of nations sundered within themselves by great accumulations of wealth at one pole and great poverty at the other.

When I visited the farmhouse in Siboney, from which Fidel and 135 valiant youth had left to storm the Moncada Barracks in 1953, I saw evidence on display that some of them had been reading Lenin. And in an exhibit of photos taken in the Sierra Maestra, I saw a picture of Castro, sitting against a tree, a long cigar jutting out of his shaggy beard, his eyes glued to a book by Karl Marx resting on his knees.

Marxism has a long history and proud traditions in Cuba. The first founder of the revolutionary student movement in the 1920's was Julio Mella, a founder also of the first Communist Party. For decades the Communists had been the leading force in the Cuban working class movement. Lázaro Peña, a black Communist, had headed the Cuban trade union movement. When a previous bloody dictator, Gerardo Machado, was overthrown by armed insurrection in 1933, Cuban workers in Las Villas province alone had taken over 36 sugar mill *centrales* and established local soviets in Nazabal, Mal Tiempo, Parque Alto and other sugar centers.

Communists also played an important role in the final overthrow of Batista and had conducted an underground struggle against him from the time he grabbed power in 1952. Carlos Rafael Rodríguez, a leader of the Partido Socialista Popular, as the old Communist party was known, was its official representative at the headquarters of Fidel in the Sierra Maestra from June 1958, to January 1959. Two other members of the PSP were military *comandantes* in the field.

Thus there was some coordination between the advancing columns of the rebel army and the urban forces of the PSP. With the aid of a powerful nationwide general strike, and between the pincer blows of guerrilla assault and local armed insurrection, the Batista regime crumbled, the bloody dictator fleeing with his personal loot.

In effect, therefore, two revolutionary vanguard forces existed and cooperated to a certain degree. The PSP was the party with great working-class traditions and the ideological spokesman for Marxism-Leninism and socialism. The July 26th movement was the democratic, anti-imperialist vanguard, which had won for itself the undisputed leadership of the military struggle. And Fidel Castro was the acknowledged leader of the revolution.

The assault on the Moncada Barracks had been the strategic turning point in the mass fight against the Batista dictatorship. Before, there had been mass opposition and resistance to the regime but no organized planning for its armed overthrow. Moncada changed this. Fidel's impassioned speech in the courtroom, "History Will Absolve Me," was a clarion call to arms. It was answered by the birth of the July 26th Movement. And when Fidel led the *Granma* landing three years later and succeeded in reaching the Sierra

Maestra, it marked the beginning of the end for the hated dictatorship.

The greatness of Fidel is that he knew that the time to act had come. He knew also that the revolution could not be made by a small handful; only by the people itself. But he had confidence that popular hatred for the regime and anti-imperialist consciousness was such that the people would respond to the call for armed struggle. A valiant handful ready to give the example, proved to be the spark that ignited the revolutionary flame.

Later, the leadership of the PSP, which in the early period of the guerrilla war had certain misgivings about its timeliness, acknowledged publicly that events had confirmed the correctness of the path pursued by Fidel. History has certainly absolved Fidel Castro.

The end of the Batista dictatorship did not mark the end of the revolution, only its new beginning. Soon difficulties arose. Liberals who had supported the overthrow of Batista were opposed to the revolution going further. They did not want his bloody henchmen brought to justice. They feared the revolutionary workers and peasants. Some were opposed to real agrarian reform. They were frightened about coming into collision with U.S. corporate interests and the U.S. government. They wanted a policy of accommodation with imperialism.

At first Fidel Castro limited his governmental role to that of head of the new revolutionary armed forces. But it soon became clear that he would have to take the helm of government because he alone had the complete confidence of the people. Later, in July 1959, differences within the government came to a head and brought about the resignation of Dr. Manuel Urrutia, as provisional President. Urrutia had sought to divide the revolutionary forces by branding all revolutionary reforms as "Communist," and charging that the Communists had undue influence within the government. He was replaced by Osvaldo Dorticós.

This development of internal division is not something new in the history of revolutions. Frederick Engels, analyzing the lessons of the German Revolution of 1848 in a series of articles in the *New York Tribune* in 1851-52, wrote, "it is the fate of all revolutions that this union of different classes, which in some degree is always the condition of any revolution, cannot subsist long. No sooner is the victory gained against the common enemy than the victors become divided among themselves. . . . It is this rapid and passionate development of class antagonisms which, in old and complicate social organisms, makes a revolution such a powerful agent of social and political progress . . . makes a nation pass in five years over more ground than it would have done in a century under ordinary circumstances." (*Germany: Revolution and Counter Revolution.*)

In the Cuban Revolution this process was accelerated by the unremitting pressure of U.S. imperialism which was determined to strangle the young revolution in its infancy, doing all in its power to aid the internal forces of counter-revolution. To protect itself and its gains, to keep from being driven back, the revolution was compelled to go ever forward, and at a fast pace.

It was compelled to go forward only because there was a leadership determined not to go back. Had, the leadership been less committed to its revolutionary principles, less daring in its view, less confident in its people, it could have been "compelled" to retreat before external and internal pressures.

A second fact accelerating the process of leftward movement was the existence of a world socialist camp, ready to give the Cuban Revolution whatever aid and support it could and with no strings attached. Blocked from the U.S. market which in the past had accounted for 85 per cent of Cuban exports, the Cuban Revolution could turn to the Soviet Union and to other socialist countries.

The same conditions that were bringing forth new internal divisions were also producing new and higher forms of unity. Millions of Cubans became even more determined to defend their revolution from Yankee imperialism, come what may. More and more Cubans began to see the integral relationship between independence and socialism.

In the past, national oppression tended to obscure the existence of class divisions and class antagonisms. But in today's world the national and class questions are closely related, for the national bourgeoisie of an oppressed nation, even if it is swept into the popular anti-imperialist struggle, tends to compromise with imperialism as soon as class tensions begin to emerge. Only with socialism can there be a unified plan of economic development and the assurance that all the resources of the nation are used for its development and not squandered on luxuries for a leisure class. Only under working-class rule, in alliance with the poor peasantry, can there be the guarantee that the revolution will know how to defend itself from external and internal foes both militarily and economically, and how to carry through the social transformation of the nation.

On April 16, 1961, speaking before the bodies of Cubans machine-gunned by U.S. planes as a prelude to the Bay of Pigs invasion of the following day, Fidel Castro proclaimed the existence of the first socialist state in the western hemisphere. The first free territory of the Americas had become the Socialist Republic of Cuba.

Once again the revolution was not over. One period had ended, another had begun. The main external foe of the revolution, the Colossus of the North, would be even more implacable toward it. Within the country, the expropriated part of the national bourgoisie would intensify its sabotage and resistance. The revolution would face new trials and tests of strength. The need for a single, unified vanguard party became more imperative.

Former differences between "old" and "new" revolutionists, often expressed along generational lines, began to disappear. The heat of the struggle had cleansed ranks of both wavering and sectarian elements; a new unity based on socialist, Marxist-Leninist principles was being built. But the organizational rift still persisted. It was impossible for one organization merely to merge into the other. A *new* party had to be formed, composed of the very best of both the July 26th and the PSP organizations.

On December 2, 1961, Fidel Castro declared, "I am a Marxist-Leninist and will be one until the day I die." He had not been one while a student at the University of Havana, he said, because he was "influenced by imperialist and reactionary propaganda against the Communists." By 1953 his political thinking had become, "more or less what it is now." But he said that he only developed into a Marxist-Leninist after he came to

power. He also called for the formation of a "United
Party of the Socialist Revolution," with membership
strictly limited to true revolutionists.

9   The New Communist Party

The unique path of the Cuban Revolution and the
development of its own singular style also left their
mark on the way in which the new Communist party
was formed and the way it functions. It is a party based
on the universal principles of Marxism-Leninism and
organized along democratic centralist lines, but the
application of these principles is distinctly Cuban.

There is great stress in Cuba today on the decisive
importance of the Communist party. In factories,
farms, dams, construction sites, cities and towns we
visited, even in some restaurants and hotels, we saw
placards proudly announcing the existence of a local
party and the recent increase in its membership. In the
Santa Clara machine-building plant, I even saw a hand-
lettered banner hanging from a rafter in the foundry
reading: "Where a Communist is born, difficulties
die!" which is certainly claiming a great deal.

Yet with all this emphasis on the importance of the
party, it is not a very large organization. According
to Blas Roca, former General Secretary of the PSP
and now a member of the new party's Secretariat, the
Communist Party of Cuba has about 55,000 members
in its ranks. I could find no published figures of party
membership; the single exception was a printed speech
by Armando Hart, Organizational Secretary of the
party, giving the membership of Havana province as
11,824.

The limited size of party membership is due to conscious policy, although there is now a determination to double its size in the current year. Were the doors to party membership thrown open to all who would join, tens of thousands would rush in overnight. But people do not just join the party in Cuba. They must first be elected to it.

Before a person can be taken into the party in Cuba he must be chosen for this honor by his fellow workers, including those who are not members of the party. His fellow workers must first pass judgment. Is he truly devoted to the revolution and ready to sacrifice for it? Is he an example of what a Communist should be? Will his membership raise or lower the prestige of the party in the eyes of the people? Only then is his membership acted upon.

This method of choosing party members, I was told, ensures that the party remains the vanguard instrument of the working class and not separate from it. It was stressed that if party members are chosen by the workers and these people also have the power to initiate proceedings to remove someone from the party's ranks, then the people will understand why there is only one political party.

With the main ideological stress being placed on moral incentives, it is evident that those belonging to the party must be exemplary in this respect. They must be the first to volunteer their services and the very last to receive individual material benefits.

What the Cuban party expects of its members is contained in one of its educational bulletins, entitled "Considerations About Ideological Work." This study guide declares: "Human and social sensitivity is the fundamental element of Communist morals. It is impossible to conceive a Communist who is not indignant at all injustice and social arbitrariness. The struggle against these constitutes the basis of Communist morality."

What a Communist should be is summarized in these words: "A Communist is an intransigent and impassioned fighter against all weaknesses. He is a rebel with cause.... One cannot be a Communist if he is not a rebel, and if he is not intransigent in the face of arbitrariness, injustice, and whatever weaknesses or errors digress or hold back society's march toward Communism.... The Communist does not struggle for a private interest, nor for a group interest. He struggles for a social interest, for the interests of all the workers. Moreover, he does not struggle for the exclusive interests of one people; his cause is that of all humanity. Internationalism is an essential ingredient of Communist morality. Without it, Communist consciousness is impossible."

To become such a communist, this educational guide stresses, each member must develop his own "rebel and heroic spirit," and must have the desire to "study, reason out and discover the solution to daily problems." He must constantly heighten his own sense of discipline and social responsibility, making heroism and self-sacrifice the distinguishing characteristics of all his work.

The decisive importance of discipline is underlined. "Communist discipline," it points out," is determined by the functional and operational needs of all society and by the identity of aspirations, principles and ideals. It is not, for this reason, a discipline founded on terror, ambition, submission, or fear. It is a discipline born from conviction and the consciousness of necessity."

Standards for Cuban party membership, as can be seen, are exceedingly high. The building of the party has been a slow, extended process. At the outset certain differences of approach arose. A number of individuals were removed from party leadership because of arbitrary, sectarian and bureaucratic methods. Fidel accused some individuals of building the party as if it were an organization *over* the people and not an organization *of* the people.

When the building of the new party began in earnest, it was organized first in the factories, the armed forces and the state farms. Here socialist consciousness and working-class revolutionary discipline were strongest. Only later was membership solicited in the ministry of education, the universities, among intellectuals, etc.

In 1969, the leadership stressed the need to rapidly increase the size of the party if it is to give effective leadership to all the varied fields of work and areas of the country. This decision to increase party membership has met with some ideological resistance. The problem was discussed quite frankly by Armando Hart in his report to a meeting of party activists, reprinted in the columns of *Granma*.

Hart points out that there is now a sizeable pool of tested workers from which party members can be drawn, industry by industry. Approximately 235,000 workers belong to the *avanzado* or *vanguardista* groups in the factories and fields. These advanced workers consciously and conscientiously participate in the planning of production and are examples of work performance and voluntary contribution of labor. In most work places the *avanzados* are considred the natural candidates for party membership.

The Union of Communist Youth, UJC, is the organization closest to the party and a ready source from which party members can be recruited. In some places we found conditions for membership in the UJC quite strict. In one, the fertilizer construction project in Cienfuegos, the party and the UJC are actually merged into one for the duration of the building effort.

Other popular mass organizations and movements exist with tens of thousands of conscious, revolutionary activists from which party members can be recruited. A popular militia involves many hundreds of thousands of people who voluntarily bear arms and stand guard to protect the revolution. The great mass movement composed of members of the Committees for Defense of the Revolution, known as the CDR, has over a million members, all dedicated to work for the revolution and organized on a block by block and community by community basis. The Federation of Cuban Women also has over a million members. An organization of poor farmers, ANAP, also exists. And there are others.

Yet the party has grown at only a snail's pace. Hart cites the figures for Havana province. At the end of 1967, the party had 11,179 members. At the end of 1968, the party had 11,824, an increase of only 645. Why this slow rate of growth?

Armando Hart's explanation is that there exists a narrow, schematic, over-zealous approach to the issue of moral consciousness. It seems, according to him, that workers look for "perfect" beings when there are only human beings. He quotes Che Guevara, "We cannot build a party of archangels." This use of Che's words against a narrow approach to the moral issue is extremely important, for it is Che who is held up as the finest example of the moral qualities a Communist should possess.

The party's Secretary of Organization warns that problems of personal conduct must be analyzed more carefully if grave injustices are not to result. Often, he says, candidates for party membership are rejected because they are brusque, outspoken, and sometimes hard to get along with. These personality traits should be criticized and combated. But, asks Hart rhetorically, what kind of party will we have if we build it only of people who never quarrel or collide? It will eliminate conflict, that is true, but it may also eliminate the party's ability to solve complex problems.

The starting point in judging each person should be political and ideological, says Hart. It should be based on "his readiness to struggle and to die for the cause of the revolution. This is the first principle to remember if we are not to fall into errors of schematism." The key to judging people should be their "revolutionary activity and conduct, their militancy and their comprehension of the line of the revolution." Only after that should personality characteristics enter into consideration, and then each case must be submitted to separate, specific examination.

In the approach to moral questions, concludes Hart, the starting point must always be an analysis of the revolutionary history and activity of the individual involved. It must be remembered that on moral questions "there intervene many existing social customs that cannot be abolished overnight, for they form part of the ideological, moral and social superstructure of society."

Thus we see two sides of the moral question as it confronts the Cuban party—great stress on morality and, simultaneously, recognition of the danger of a puritanical, sectarian approach.

At the enterprises we visited I asked about party and Communist youth membership. At some of the new, more important projects, the percentage of party members was high. At the Tri-Continental automatic loading dock at Cienfuegos, for example, there were 40 members in the Party and 12 in the UJC. The total work force, divided into three eight-hour shifts and one relief shift, was 240. One hundred and forty of these were *vanguardistas*. The highest percentage of party members was at the Cienfuegos fertilizer construction site. Here, of 1,583 workers there were 533 party and 634 UJC members combined into one organization. The reason for this exceedingly high percentage of Communists is that the whole brigade was established as a "Communist Construction Brigade."

In the machine-building shop at Santa Clara, the most important of its kind in the country, approximately 1,700 workers were employed, of which some 200 were in the party and UJC. However in the very important sugar mill, El Central Venezuela, of 1,500 workers only 74 were in the party and 67 in the UJC; however, 354 were *vanguardistas*.

How these data compare with national averages can be seen by two sets of figures given in Armando Hart's report. In all of Cuba, 8,340 workers are employed in the electrical industry. Of these, 404, or a little less than five per cent, are members of the party. In the extremely important machine-building industry, 12,743 workers are employed. A total of 367, or less than three per cent, are in the party.

10   Cuba and World Communism

The Cuban party is as integral a part of the world communist movement, as Cuba is of the world socialist camp. While a part of this world movement and a staunch defender of its unity, Cuba has maintained its own independent position on a number of ideological and political questions. At times it has also publicly voiced criticisms of policies and practices in the world communist movement with which it has disagreed.

This is not the occasion to discuss at length or in depth the nature of some of these differences, *per se*, for these are complex and in constant flux. I shall limit myself therefore to certain impressions gained in Cuba of its approach to the problems of the world movement.

I spoke with Carlos Rafael Rodríguez about some of these matters on the eve of his departure for the Meeting of Communist Parties held in Moscow in June 1969. He told me that the Cuban party had not changed its views. It still felt that the world meeting should enter far more critically into a discussion of the real state of affairs in sections of the international movement and the ideological and political differences within its ranks. Despite the fact that the conference would not do this, the Cuban party had decided to participate as observer, so that its absence would not be misinterpreted and utilized by imperialism as a weapon to divide the world movement.

Rafael said that despite continuing differences on certain ideological question, the Cuban party and the Cuban people feel very warm and close to the Soviet party and the Soviet people. The Soviet Union had fulfilled all its obligations toward Cuba, he said. Without its military aid and economic support revolutionary Cuba could not have survived.

Cuba's relations with China are formal and by no means close. The trouble, he said, lies with the Chinese leaders. They use a crude yardstick to measure friendship. Either you are 100 per cent with them or you are considered to be 100 per cent against them. Nothing in between is tolerated.

Some of the Cuban party's differences with other parties in the world movement relate to the way in which the question of peaceful coexistence has been posed at times, which, according to the Cuban leadership, has given rise here and there to pacifist and reformist illusions. The Cuban Party has differences with other parties of socialist countries over whether moral or material incentives should get the prime emphasis in the building of socialism. It has differences on the question of guerrilla warfare and armed struggle in general and their relationship to peaceful, parliamentary forms of struggle.

The Cuban party agrees that the struggle for peace is of paramount importance and that toward this end the unity of the most diverse forces should be sought. But it also holds that since peace is part of the battle against imperialism, revolutionists must set as their strategic goal the complete defeat and elimination of imperialism itself. The Cuban party also believes that there is a tendency in Latin America to see only the danger of military, reactionary dictatorship, while underestimating the role of liberal reformism as a tool of U.S. imperialism. It sees reformism as the main danger in the working-class movement in the developed capitalist countries, and holds that with the aid of a labor aristocracy the bourgeoisie has had some success in integrating the workers' movement into the system of capitalist domination. Whether the Cuban party is right or wrong in its views, it can readily be seen that it is addressing itself to vital questions under discussion and review throughout the world Communist movement.

Because of its great concentration on domestic problems, it would be a mistake to think that the Cuban Revolution is now only concerned with its own economic development and is losing some of its internationalist spirit and perspective. I saw no signs of this in Cuba. A whole new generation is being taught that Cuba will never be satisfied with its own transformation into a luxuriant island paradise, so long as other peoples remain exploited and oppressed and live in poverty. At the same time, it is recognized that Cuban victories in the war against underdevelopment can be a great inspiration to all oppressed people to follow.

The Cuban party has not changed its view that other peoples must be ready to employ arms if they mean to become free. The general approach to the Che Guevara tragedy in Bolivia is identical with that taken toward the Moncada Barracks assault. Yes, I was told, it had not achieved its immediate tactical objectives. Yes, there were certain errors in judgment involved. But it was not a failure from a longer, deeper strategic view.

How strongly Cubans feel on this matter can be seen by the way in which Carlos Rafael answered a question about Che's "failure" to a world press conference in Lima, Peru, of which previous mention has been made. When it comes to success and failure, Rafael said, Cubans do not consider that José Martí failed because he died in 1895, 64 years before the Cuban Revolution triumphed. He continued:

"And in this sense, we consider that the victors in
Bolivia are not the living but the dead. The living believe they are alive but they are dead. History is never
going to speak of the military assassins of Che Guevara and of those who instigated the assassination, but
it is going to speak of Che Guevara and his companions.

"We believe that if the alternative could have been
presented to Che Guevara whether to continue living,
or the happy prospect of producing in the world—not
only in Latin America but in all the world—so dramatic
an impact upon the consciousness of hundreds of
thousands of youth, he would have chosen death voluntarily.

"For this reason, in the same way that we do not la-
ment having lost José Martí, one of the foremost writers of Latin America, . . . we know that we lost him
[Che] in something we consider a victory for the revolutionaries of Latin America."

In other words, the Cuban view of Che Guevara's
"failure" is similar to our own estimate of John
Brown's "failure" at Harper's Ferry.

11   Cuban Democracy

Castro had promised the Cuban people restoration of
the 1940 constitution. He kept his word. But the revolutionary broom did not stop at this reform. It swept
clean the entire, corrupt, bureaucratic state apparatus.
In the language of Marx and Lenin, the revolution
"broke up" and "smashed" the old state machine.

The standing army of Batista was defeated in battle
and then totally destroyed. The people were given

arms and the old army as well as the police force were replaced with the rebel army and a popular militia. Hundreds of Batista hangmen were brought to revolutionary justice, tried in open court by the people themselves; those found guilty of wholesale, cold-blooded murder paid the full penalty. On January 6, 1959, only six days after the fall of Batista, the new government declared Cuba's Congress dissolved and removed all office holders, whether elected or appointed, including governors, congressmen, mayors and aldermen.

Even within the framework of the old bourgeois constitution a new type of revolutionary state was emerging. Lenin had described this new state as "one in which a standing army and police divorced from the people are *replaced* by the direct arming of the people themselves." (Lenin, "Tasks of Proletariat in Our Revolution," *Collected Works,* Vol 24, p. 68.)

In other words, although the Cuban Revolution had not yet become socialist in character and the means of production were still in the hands of the capitalist class, Cuban state power was no longer in these hands. There was no longer a "privileged bureaucracy" or "an army divorced from the people." And it is precisely this feature, Lenin had said, which distinguishes the new revolutionary state from the old bourgeois state.

Thanks to this thorough-going quality of the democratic revolution against Batista, the later socialist stage of the revolution was carried through with relative ease and free of bloodshed. But the restored liberal, bourgeois democratic constitution could no longer fit the needs of the new proletarian state.

Socialist society requires its own legal framework. For the past eight years the Cubans have been at work constructing one. But they have been in no hurry to institutionalize their revolution too rapidly. When it comes to this matter they prefer to make haste slowly. Thus no new constitution has been drafted as yet and there is no congress or system of national elections.

There are a number of reasons for this. The first has to do with the chronic state of siege that Cuba finds itself in *viz a viz* the United States. The economic blockade imposed by the United States is a form of unrelenting warfare, meant to strangle the revolution into submission. Nor can the Cubans forget for even a single moment that a powerful U.S. military base still occupies their soil at Guantanamo, and that U.S. money, arms and drill sergeants still train mercenary troops in clandestine camps in Guatemala, Nicaragua, Panama and elsewhere for purposes of a Cuban invasion. And there are also crisis contingencies that arise from the internal struggle to overcome economic and cultural underdevelopment.

But there is another important reason. A new class in power requires a new type of governmental structure. This cannot be a mere patched-up, even if more radical, version of the old state power. Nor can it be invented or established overnight. It must arise from life itself, from the new economic and social reality and the new initiative of the millions, for the first time experiencing the meaning of self-government. As stressed by both Engels and Lenin, the socialist state must be a state which is "no longer a state in the proper sense of the word."

How to build such a state, while at the same time defending the revolution from its external and internal foes, is the big question. Because there are contradictions involved in the very attempt to accomplish this, care must be taken not to institutionalize or freeze forms of rule that tomorrow may become obstacles to their own dismantlement.

These were the main reasons given me for the slowness in drafting a constitution and the fluidity in governmental forms that one finds in different parts of the island. I talked with no one who missed the lack of a congress or parliament. I do not say there are none, but I did not meet them. The people I met, and not only the responsible party and government officials, but also average citizens, tended to equate parliament and national elections with corrupt bourgeois politics. We had elections, I was told, even under Batista. Those elected were no more representative of the people than Batista, who also had himself "elected" after his military coup in 1952.

I was also reminded that the puppet dictatorships in Latin America also have parliaments and regularly go through the deception of national elections. There was frank admission that Cuba today is governed by an open, revolutionary working-class dictatorship whose legality is derived from the conscious, organized and armed might of the people. Democracy, I was told, is the daily *direct* involvement of the people in governing themselves.

The reluctance of Cubans to rush into institutionalizing their revolution should be understood by North Americans who know something about our own national history. Eleven years separated the Declaration of Independence from the Constitutional Convention of 1887, and 13 years from the first national election. Yet the American Revolution did not alter the basic structure of class rule, bourgeois before the revolution and bourgeois after. The rising bourgeoisie of the 13 colonies wanted to be sovereign in its own home, refusing to continue to pay tribute to a foreign master. The revolution succeeded in ending British oppression of the colonies but made no pretense at ending class oppression within the colonies. The black slaves remained in chains. The poor whites, indentured or "free," remained exploited.

The Cuban Revolution, in contrast, was a mighty social upheaval in which *los de abajo* rose to the top and *los de arriba* sank to the bottom. Nor is Cuba a huge continent separated from her imperial foe by a mighty ocean and the slowness of sail-power. It is a small island right under the nose of U.S. naval, jet and rocket power.

12   Where Black and White Unite

Miguel, the student of Havana University who accompanied me across Cuba, was dark-skinned. Had he lived in the United States I would have referred to him as black or Negro. But Miguel did not consider himself as such. He was Cuban. There are black Cubans, of course, but they are not just dark or brown, they are *black*. On this distinction hangs a tale that tells a great deal about the historic development of race relations in Cuba as contrasted to the United States.

There had been racial discrimination before the revolution and sharp color distinctions. The ruling class prided itself on its "pure" white, Castilian stock. Next came the great mass of mulattos of various shades of color. Finally there were the blacks, those who were closer to "pure" African in color. This latter category was a minority of the population, most living in rural areas, especially in Oriente province.

Over and above color distinctions that divided the Cuban people, there were also certain historic factors that drew them together. The Cuban people experienced in common their oppression as a colony of Spain and then as a colony and semi-colony of the United States.

All Cubans shared in the history of struggle against foreign domination. The greatest national heroes of Cuba, the two martyrs of the war against Spain, are José Martí, white, and Antonio Maceo, black. Memories of both have been kept alive, honored and revered by *all* Cuban patriots, regardless of color.

Martí and Maceo are like Thomas Jefferson and George Washington in U.S. history. Martí was the greatest intellectual leader of the war against Spain and for independence; Maceo, its greatest military leader.

However, one cannot really compare Martí and Maceo with Jefferson and Washington, for there is not the same emotional attachment on the part of the people of the United States to their war against Britain as there is by the Cubans to their independence struggle. Ours was over in seven years of fighting that took place nearly 200 years ago. The Cuban military war for independence went on from 1868 to 1898 against Spain and then turned into a protracted struggle for freedom from U.S. domination. The war begun by Martí and Maceo was finally won on January 1, 1959, ninety-one years later.

Even under Cuban slavery there were factors at work quite different from those in the United States. Claude Lightfoot, in his book *Ghetto Rebellion to Black Liberation* (New York, 1968) devotes two chapters to the race issue in Cuba and how it is being solved under socialism. He makes the important observation that slavery was established in Cuba against a background of a dying feudal system in Spain, while in the United States it arose and developed in context of a rising capitalist society. The slave codes in Cuba were more lenient and it was easier for slaves to procure their freedom. Thus there was a far greater percentage of free blacks in the total population. In 1861, according to Lightfoot, there were 748,000 whites and 613,000 colored, of which 213,000 (or almost 35 per cent) were free.

While identifying with the Cuban national struggle against colonialism and for independence, the black man in Cuba continued to retain his own special African cultural heritage, expressed in music, dance and religious customs. And these have had a decided influence on Cuban culture as a whole.

For these reasons, and because the majority of Cuban working people are dark-skinned, either mulatto or black, the working class of Cuba was not as saturated with the poison of racism as that of the United States. Only the aristocratic upper crust gloried in its whiteness or, more accurately, its pinkness.

The extent to which racism has not been a major factor in the ranks of the Cuban working class is symbolized by its greatest labor hero and martyr, Jesús Menéndez. A black, sugar mill union leader, Menéndez was murdered during a strike in 1947.

The elected leader of the Cuban trade union movement in the thirties and forties was also an Afro-Cuban, Lázaro Peña. It is as if the leader of the AFL-CIO in the United States were a black worker instead of the racist George Meany.

The fact that Menéndez and Peña were both Communists says a great deal about the level of class consciousness and political understanding of the Cuban working-class movement. Nor is it accidental that, as anti-communism and racism come together in the top leadership of the U.S. labor movement, the opposite is true in Cuba.

During my stay in Oriente province I discussed the color question with a number of black workers and leaders. They all pointed to numerous examples of discrimination before the revolution. They did the hardest work for the lowest pay. Their children had the poorest educational facilities, and in the rural areas none whatsoever. They had no health facilities and, where these existed, no means to pay for them.

"What are your problems today?" I asked. "They are the same as everyone else's," was a typical reply. "In fact, we feel we have gained more from the revolution than anyone else. Because we were the poorest of the poor, more of our children have now been given scholarships for higher learning. Also, we are now leaders in the party, army, militia and in industry."

"Do you not still face certain discrimination?"

"Well," came the reply, "sometimes we bump into individual cases of prejudice, but these are the exception. When it comes to our rights and to opportunities, we now have them in full."

This was the typical reply of black people — black, that is, in the Cuban use of the term. As for the larger number of in-between shades of color, I could find no one who would agree that there is any prejudice whatsoever. In fact, Miguel used to say I was trying to find a needle in a haystack.

Adjusting to a situation in which there were blacks but no black movement is a problem faced by nearly all U.S. visitors to Cuba who are sensitive to the prob-

lem of race relations. Some have even concluded that
the Cubans are insensitive to the problem of racial
prejudice and discrimination. They find it difficult to
understand how Cuba's black people can have equality
without a special movement, a special press, and their
own black leaders speaking for the blacks. But black
leaders in Cuba are not just leaders of blacks, or of
blacks and mulattos, but leaders of all Cubans.

Racism is not the normal state of human nature, but
the abnormal state of a class society, a means to divide
people in the interests of capital's rule and greater
profits. Cuba is an inspiring example that black and
white can live together in peace and harmony.

13   New Laws and People's Courts

Blas Roca is chairman of a commission now at work
on a new constitution, but a first draft is still a considerable way off. Instead, the commission has been
preparing piecemeal a series of new laws which, when
completed, will establish a system of *de facto* revolutionary legality.

One of the new laws of which they are very proud
covers social security. For the first time in Cuban history, men and women reaching 65 years of age will receive government pensions, 60 pesos a month. Thousands of meetings were held all over Cuba in which
every aspect of the proposed law was discussed and
amendments offered. When the final draft was ap-
proved by the Council of Ministers, it was submitted
for endorsement to a huge rally of hundreds of thousands of people in Havana's Plaza of the Revolution.

Asking an immense multitude to pass final judgment on a piece of legislation is not necessarily democracy, and could easily be the opposite. But I was assured that this law had really been discussed thoroughly everywhere and that the demonstration was more in the nature of a popular celebration.

In the gradual elaboration of a new governmental structure, special care is being taken to prevent the formation of a new bureaucratic stratum separated from the people. In a speech delivered some time ago, Fidel told the Cuban people that they had two enemies —imperialism and bureaucracy. And, he said, long after imperialism is dead the problem of bureaucracy will still remain as a vestige of old class society and a reminder that communist society is not yet fully achieved.

Blas Roca described the court system that has emerged as an example of the new approach to democracy. The lower courts are made up of three members each. These are elected on a geographic and population basis, community by community. The judges of these courts are ordinary men and women without formal legal training. They are workers, farmers, professionals, housewives, or students living in the community. They continue to work at their usual jobs and sit in court in the evening after work. They receive no remuneration for this public service, only the honor of having been entrusted by their neighbors with this great responsibility.

Minor infringements of the law are usually handled out of court. If a worker in a shop is caught stealing, his shopmates discuss the matter with him and decide whether it can be handled by reprimand and censure, or is serious enough to refer to the courts.

When a case is put on the docket of the court, one of the three judges is assigned to the task or preliminary investigation. He interviews the accused, speaks with his family and neighbors, and becomes thoroughly acquainted with the specific human problems involved. When the case is finally heard, relatives, neighbors and friends can attend and have the right to be heard.

This entire lower judicial system is being built without a paid bureaucracy, depending entirely upon the voluntary participation of ordinary citizens. In this way, it was stressed, the people learn to govern themselves directly and without a bureaucratic caste. The higher appeal courts are also being structured on the same principle, although these cover larger geographic areas and require judges with greater experience.

How well this system works I do not know from personal observation. Philadelphia lawyers may not be needed, and Wall Street lawyers certainly not, but there still is need for some form of legal adviser to the defendant as well as to the judge. Every person charged with crime in Cuba has the right to legal counsel and to be defended in court by a lawyer at absolutely no cost to himself. He also has the right to argue his own case, should that be his preference. The attempt is to do away with legal mumbo-jumbo and with the conscious obfuscation of the law which is so terrifying to people, especially poor people, in capitalist society. In Cuba the "majesty of the law" is removed from its pedestal over the people and placed directly in their hands to render simple justice.

Let no one draw the conclusion from this that the Cubans are soft on crime. While trying specifically to evaluate each separate crime and its cause, the Cubans are exceedingly harsh on incorrigibles and on certain types of crimes. They consider crime as a natural by-product of capitalist society with its oppression, exploitation, unemployment and racial discrimination. They believe it to be unnatural for Cuba, where jobs are plentiful, equal opportunity exists for all, and there is no exploiting class.

Under conditions in which most Cuban people must work hard and endure certain hardships to help defeat the blockade and to overcome underdevelopment, they are completely intolerant of any form of parasitism, of people who make a profession of living off another person's toil.

How severe they can be is seen by Law 1098. This law, adopted in 1963, permits the death penalty for certain types of crimes. Three specific kinds are listed: the entrance of someone's home for purposes of robbery, posing as an officer or government representative for purposes of fraud, and the use of children and minors for criminal purposes.

Since the adoption of this law there has been a softening of its application. Its net effect has been a reduction in these specific types of crimes. But according to Pedro Pupo Perez, the Vice-Minister of Internal Affairs, the same criminal elements only varied their mode of operation, switching to other types of crimes. The results, therefore, have been the same as in all past history. The threat of capital punishment has never been a successful deterrent to crime.

Delinquency and crime in Cuba is small compared to the United States. In 1968, 28,000 crimes "against property" were recorded for all of Cuba. In the United States, for the same year, the Department of Justice reports 4.5 million "serious crimes." Taking into account the difference in population between Cuba and

the United States, this would still make the crime rate
in the United States more than six times that of Cuba.
Two U.S. citizens who have lived in Cuba for the past
eight years told me they had never heard of a mugging
or act of violence on the streets of Havana. They said
that women and children safely walk the streets at any
hour, even the early hours of the morning when the
streets are dark and dimly lit.

14   Local Power

In many cities and towns, I noticed placards in store
windows or on building walls bearing the words, *Poder
Local.* I soon learned what Local Power in Cuba meant.

Poder Local is the name of the municipal or regional
people's assembly that performs the combined function of city council and local administration. The placards in store windows signify that the given business
is operated under the jurisdiction of the local government. When the revolutionary offensive took over the
remaining small businesses it was these peoples' *Poder
Local* councils that assumed the responsibility for their
operation and management. All stores and enterprises
that serve purely local needs are owned and run lo-
cally and not by national agencies.

Poder Local, or local government, is composed of
ordinary men and women directly elected by the people. It carries the full responsibility for the administration of local services. Cooperating with *Poder Local*
are a network of diverse peoples' organizations that
crisscross and reach every section of the population
and frequently overlap in function. Functioning on

different levels of consciousness, these organizations serve the people and the revolution in different fields of work and in diverse ways. They all aim to involve the people directly in problems of self-government and are an exciting feature of Cuban democracy.

In many ways the most important of these organizations are the Committees for Defense of the Revolution, CDR, whose members are known as *Cederistas*. It is hard to say how many Cubans are members of the CDR. I have seen figures ranging from one million to as high as three million.

The CDR committees exist all over Cuba, on a village level in the rural areas, block by block in the cities and towns. Comprising conscious, dedicated defenders of the revolution, the CDR is a combination civilian defense, political education and public service. It is ready to respond to every need — the personal need of a neighbor, the social needs of the community, or the needs of the country for, say, sugarcane *macheteros*.

If a neighbor on the block needs indoor plumbing, or the peasants of a nearby village want their earthen floors turned into cement ones, the *Cederistas* are there to help. They plant trees and gardens; paint schools, nurseries or homes; repair leaky roofs and faucets. They see that all children are vaccinated against smallpox and polio; that people who have overcome illiteracy continue their education; that the parents of children who are absentee problems in school are visited and advised; that incidents of crime or juvenile delinquency are dealt with as matters of common community concern.

To help the country meet essential needs without the expenditure of additional foreign currency, *Cederistas* collect empty medicine flasks and bottles, old rags and paper, and even old postage stamps that can be sold abroad as collector's items. In the four month period, January through April 1969, the *Cederistas* collected more than 23 million vials and bottles, saving about $415,000 in foreign currency. They also collected more than 2,710 tons of paper and cardboard, saving the country about $400,000.

The CDRs are the arms and legs of the revolution and the local governments. They also participate actively in the leadership of government and often take the initiative on important questions. For example, the CDRs are credited with first raising the problem of small businesses becoming centers for self-enrichment and counter-revolution. By their intimate, close contact with the people, they know what is going on, what people think, what their gripes are, and seek solution to problems themselves while referring those that cannot be solved that way to higher echelons of responsibility.

In the same four-month period of January to April, more than 67,000 classes were organized by the CDR, on local, municipal and regional levels. The CDRs were also involved in the exceedingly important work of organizing 7,618 public assemblies, where thousands of men and women of a given region or city discussed the most important problems of their community. Where answers were not immediately forthcoming or did not have a clear concensus, they were referred for further consideration to future gatherings.

Thus the CDR has become one of the most potent organizations of the new Cuba. It plays a key role in *Poder Local* and is manned by volunteer workers who give of their free, afterwork time. In *Poder Local* activities alone, 1,097,000 *Cederistas* participated in the

first four months of 1969. The CDR continues to grow.
In the same four-month period, 2,051 new base committees were established and 128,987 new members
enrolled.

15   Untying the Other Hand

Not far from the city of Santa Clara is a resort village
built in typical Indian style, but with all modern con-
veniences, and used as a place for workers' vacations.
Canayes is spacious and picturesque, its large round
cottages thatched with banana and palm leaves.

I spent a night at this village resort, filled to near
capacity with young honeymooners. At the breakfast
table the next morning we were joined by a middle-
aged woman from Santa Clara who was to show us
around. She was from the *Federacion de Mujeres
Cubanas,* the large, popular woman's organization of
Cuba. One of the first things she proudly showed us
was mile after mile of new forests, planted in the past
few years as seedlings by the members of the women's
federation.

The FMC has an immense responsibility: to untie
the "other hand" in the building of the new socialist
society, the hand of Cuba's women. This is an absolute
necessity if the Cuban Revolution is to achieve full
fruition and Cuban women their own, full emancipation.

The problem of achieving women's complete liberation is not a problem of women alone. It means overcoming the traditional prejudices of men, which in
Cuba as in all countries, most especially those of semi-

feudal and colonial backgrounds, are deeply ingrained and extremely difficult to dislodge. The insidious pervasive *machismo* mentality cannot be fought by the women alone. It must be fought by all conscious revolutionary forces. But this battle cannot be won unless the women themselves pick up the cudgels in their own behalf. The FMC is the indispensable organization toward this end.

As long as man is the only breadwinner in the family and his wife the household servant doing his chores and raising the children, she will remain subordinate to him and both their outlooks will reflect this relationship. To tear woman's apron strings from the kitchen stove, to bring her out of the home into the world as an independent human being capable of earning her own living, is the most important single step in overcoming the mentality of the past.

Emancipating women from the kitchen is only one step toward full emancipation. A new obstacle looms — the double burden of working for a living and still doing the same household chores. The struggle is prolonged and complicated as can be seen from typical interviews with women by "missionaries" from the FMC, who discussed with them the possibility of their going to work. The responses were printed in *Mujeres,* the FMC's popular women's magazine:

One young women bitterly complains, "We are going to marry in December. He does not want me to work. He says, 'I am a revolutionary and I work for you and for me.' And when I tell him I am going to do voluntary work on Sundays, he says, 'No, you are not going.' Then I have to go secretly. He does not want me to go out alone and even prohibits his own sister from working. He is involved in everything, but he does not permit me to do anything. It is as if he alone made the revolution.''

Another respondent, Iris, is 19 years old. She lives in Versalles. She has eight brothers and sisters and the family lives only on her father's earnings. "I want to work," Iris says, "but my fiance does not let me."

Oscar on the other hand, is a soldier who understands the "necessity of women working." At least so he says. But, he adds, "I am going to marry at the end of the year and I would not want her to work so that she can take care of my needs." Oscar is finally convinced that his revolutionary duty is to let his wife work. The girl, pretty, intelligent, capable, listens passively to all this, says nothing, and only her expression betrays her happiness, "Oscar will let me work."

In each of these instances the problem of the woman is really the problem of the man. It is not that she does not want to work, but that he does not want her to and she has not yet emancipated herself from the slave mentality that his word is her law. However, this too is changing. *Mujeres* interviewed a woman factory worker: "I feel very proud of being a woman and a worker. How can a woman say, 'If only my husband would let me work'? Woman! What is this business of a man not letting his wife work? That may have been well for colonial or cave times, but for now, no!"

In 1964, only 282,069 women were gainfully employed in all of Cuba. Four years later this total rose to 371,069, an increase of about 32 per cent, but less than 90,000 in absolute terms.

Since then the tasks of enlisting women for work and combatting male prejudices have been undertaken in greater earnest and with greater success. The party's leadership set a goal of adding 100,000 women to the labor force in 1969. In the ten-month period from November 1968 to August 1969, 94,249 additional women went to work, a major breakthrough. In ten months as much was attained as in the previous four years. The goal set for 1975 is one million women gainfully employed. If the same rate of progress is maintained this objective can be reached.

The results obtained in recent months must be credited in large part to the work of the FMC. Its members personally visited nearly 400,000 homes and spoke with unmarried young women and their parents and with wives and husbands. Where problems of children, illness or continuing education existed, no attempt to recruit workers was made. Still, three out of four of the women eligible for work could not be convinced.

It is recognized, of course, that women, even those who are anxious to work, do have special problems. They cannot shirk their responsibilities as mothers, for these are not only personal but also social responsibilities. A significant number of women who enter production for the first time quit their jobs when they meet their first difficulties.

The FMC therefore is also concerned with helping to create conditions which will enable women to continue working. A network of *Circulos Infantiles,* child nurseries, has been established in towns and cities across Cuba. We visited the *Circulo Infantil* at Mayari Arriba, the town outside of which Raul Castro had his headquarters as *comandante* of the Second Guerrilla Front. This nursery takes care of 150 children from 45 days to six years of age. One section takes care of the infants, the other children from 19 months to six years. There are facilities for children to sleep in the nursery overnight if mothers are engaged in night work. Pre-

Nursery school children at play. The slogans on the wall: Long Live our Socialist Revolution! Long Live World Peace! Long Live Proletarian Internationalism! Long Live the Worker-Peasant Alliance!

school education begins at four, and at six the children start going to regular school.

The FMC has also organized women into Mutual Aid Brigades that assist one another wherever collective effort or individual assistance is required. Among farm women alone, 3,403 Mutual Aid Brigades have been formed.

Forty-three thousand members of the FMC attend special schools to raise their educational level and to train them for leadership. Over 40,000 other women attend special courses in dressmaking. Vilma Espin, President of the Federation of Cuban Women, says that these dressmaking courses are concerned with more than sewing. "Their studies include political and cultural subjects, and these comrades also participate in volunteer work through their respective school."

Vilma Espin told the FMC Congress that the membership had reached more than 1,132,000 and is growing more rapidly than in any period of its nine years of existence. In 1968 FMC membership increased by 197,810; and in the year between August 23, 1968, and August 23, 1969, and August 23, 1969, the anniversary date of its birth, it grew by 152,000 members.

The struggle for women's full emancipation is protracted, but the existence and growth of the *Federacion de Mujeres Cubanas* is a guarantee that it will continue until won. It is also a guarantee that Cuba's deft, other hand will be fully employed in the building of the new society.

16   The Campesinos Organize

Nearly every farmer who own his own land is a member of the *Asociacion Nacional de Agricultores Pequeños,* ANAP. This is the great mass organization of *campesinos.* Through ANAP the farmers are made aware of national planning, especially for agriculture, and its meaning for them. They discuss their relationship to national goals, how to pool resources for the most economical use of farm equipment, how to assist one another at harvest time, and how to coordinate what the small farmer is doing with the large state farms in the area.

In Las Villas province, for example, 95.8 per cent of farm owners are members of ANAP. Of these, 93.3 per cent are organized in 633 credit and service cooperatives, from which they receive technical assistance, credit, seeds and fertilizer on a collective basis. In some places the cooperatives own farm machinery such as tractors, turbines and fumigators. These are bought from the common fund and owned collectively by the members of the cooperative.

Members of ANAP receive material and technical assistance from INRA, the National Institute of Agrarian Reform. From the National Bank they receive credits for either production or investment purposes. Credits for production are used to cover the harvesting costs and are paid back upon sale of the harvest. Credits for investment go for the expansion of the cultivated area and for purchase of livestock and equipment. These credits are given for a period of from three to seven years. The bank charges no interest whatsoever. In cases where harvests are lost, as was true when hurricane Flora struck Cuba a few years ago, debts are canceled.

ANAP has also cooperated with the CDR and the Women's Federation in the establishment of a network of Mutual Aid Brigades. Farmers can assist one another whenever help is called for, or come to the aid of a nearby state farm at planting or harvest time.

Where small farmers wish to sell their land, INRA has a program which enables farmers to get payment in one of three different ways: direct immediate cash, on an installment basis, or a pension plan which provides from 40 to 120 pesos monthly. The overwhelming majority of small farmers who sell their land to the government prefer the pension plan, for they are of advanced years and seek to ensure a steady income when they can no longer work.

ANAP is the key organization through which the hundreds of thousands of farmers who till their own soil are brought into effective alliance with the working class. It is one of the extremely important organizations of revolutionary Cuba.

17   Industrial Democracy

At each industrial enterprise we visited, I asked about trade union organization and membership. Everywhere I was told that there is a union, membership in it is voluntary and that nearly all workers are union members.

There was also evidence everywhere of the existence and important role of the Advanced Workers'

Movement, the *avanzados* In two of the plants I visited, meetings of *avanzados* on a department level were in progress. They were discussing problems of production and personnel.

In addition, still another form of labor organization exists, the Labor or Work Council, which has become an important new instrument for democracy at the point of production.

The Labor Council does not run the plant; it is not the plant administration. Nor is it concerned with the sharing of profits, as is true of the Labor Councils in Yugoslavia, for example. The Labor Council in Cuba is elected by the workers in each place of work and, according to Jorge Risquet, Minister of Labor, is "an irreplaceable organization for administering labor justice, for preventing any arbitrary action on the part of the administration and for maintaining work discipline."

All disputes between workers and management that cannot be resolved on the spot by the Labor Council are referred to regional Appeals Commissions, and if still not resolved, to a National Board of Review. In the past two years the number of cases referred to the Appeals Commissions declined by two-thirds, and those referred to the Review Board declined by half. This means that the factory Labor Councils are succeeding in settling most labor disputes on the spot.

Every worker who has a grievance has the right to submit it to the Appeals Commission if he is dissatisfied with the local verdict. Only one out of every 550 workers does so. In transportation and in public health, however, individual appeals are three times the national average for reasons not yet ascertained.

Only 11 per cent of the labor claims relate to wages. Most claims arise from on-the-job work relations and from absenteeism and charges of negligence. The reason for the low percentage of wage disputes, according to Labor Minister Risquet, is that there is now a more uniform wage pattern and the workers know that "as economic development permits, decisions on wage increases will be submitted to worker assemblies."

A measuring rod of the difference between socialist and capitalist morality is to be seen in the approach of the Labor Councils to the problems of absenteeism and poor work performance. In the United States, for example, absenteeism is solved simply — by firing the worker. In socialist Cuba, however, suspension of employment is frowned upon. Firing a worker, Risquet stressed, is to condemn him to idleness, besides harming his family. While this is permissable in incorrigible cases of absenteeism, the Minister of Labor advises the Labor Councils and the Appeals Commissions to "refrain from applying these sanctions."

"Sanctions," he adds, "must be the last resort. Education and reeducation through collective criticism and the help of other workers are the basic weapons in this struggle, which, by the way, will be a long one." It will be long also because the work force itself constantly changes in composition, more recently augmented by thousands of small business proprietors and by individuals who are not accustomed to work discipline.

In cases of poor work performance, capitalist employers will either resort to outright firing or, at the very minimum, to wage penalties. The system of piecework pay is based on this principle. But it is rejected as a solution in Cuba. Risquet discusses this problem too.

"Discounting wages is an economic sanction that is ineffective when applied to people with higher incomes than needed. When applied to workers with limited incomes it hurts the family budget and the children suffer through no fault of their own. Besides being ineffective, these sanctions do not help to form the new man, to take his mind off money or to eradicate the notion that one can buy one's way out of fulfilling a social duty."

He recommends that the law permitting monetary penalties be altered and, until then, not be enforced. The answer Risquet sees to poor work performance and lack of work discipline is the constant improvement in the functioning of the Labor Councils and the further growth of the Advanced Workers' Movement. He believes that through a process of moral example coupled with persuasion, criticism and education, all workers can be won in time to a new kind of socialist work discipline arising not from compulsion but from increased social awareness.

18   Freedom

How do the Cubans deal with freedom of speech and cultural expression? I found an atmosphere in which ideological differences were neither frowned upon nor repressed. People discussed the pros and cons of extremely controversial questions. Even in respect to sensitive themes like moral incentives, I found more than one point of view freely expressed. The same is

true of differences within the world communist movement, such as whether Che Guevara erred in Bolivia
and other equally touchy subjects.

Pensamiento Critico (Critical Thought), a magazine
published by the Philosophy Department of the University of Havana, performs the function of providing
challenging material to sharpen the thinking of Cubans
concerned with theoretical and ideological controversy. It carries articles of authors from all over the
world who may or may not be Marxist-Leninists and
with whose points of view the editors may or may not
agree. Recent issues have featured articles by people
as far apart in their views as André Gorz, Jean-Paul
Sartre, Roger Garaudy, Daniel Cohn-Bendit, Ernest
Mandel, Carl Davidson, Eric Hobsbawm, Herbert
Marcuse, Monty Johnstone and Vo Nguyen Giap.

All forms of artistic expression are permissable, so
long as they do not become a cloak for counter-revolu-
tionary propaganda and activity. The official army
magazine, *Verde Olivo,* has sharply criticized certain
cultural and intellectual writings which it considers to
be objectively hostile to the revolution.

In the interview with Carlos Rafael Rodríguez in
Lima, Peru, foreign correspondents asked him questions about cultural freedom and made specific in-
quiries about the writer, Humberto Padilla. Padilla, a
leading Cuban poet, had written pieces that could be
considered hostile to the revolution. More recently
he had submitted a book of poetry in a literary contest
organized by the National Union of Writers and Artists of Cuba. The majority of the jury chosen to select
the winner was composed of foreign intellectuals. The
jury gave first prize to Padilla's entry, *Outside of the
Game.* Whether this was done with political malice

aforethought is not known, but the Cuban Union of Writers and Artists strongly disagreed with the choice. It did not believe the book represented the best of current Cuban literature.

But, said Carlos Rafael, the book was not banned; it was published in an unlimited edition. Its Foreword contains the statement of the jury selecting it for first prize. In a separate Prologue, however, the National Union of Writers and Artists explains why it disagrees with the choice. This is the only "sanction" that took place; nothing more. The reader is left to judge for himself. The Padilla book is circulated in Cuba and was sent abroad for publication there as well. Summing up, Carlos Rafael told the newsmen, "We have no fear of ideological confrontation, you can rest assured of that."

How then does one explain the severity with which the so-called "microfaction," headed by Aníbal Escalante, was treated two years ago?

Escalante, a former leader of the PSP with many years of revolutionary activity, was found guilty of a criminal offense against the revolution and sentenced to 15 years in prison. Yet his differences were ideological and political in character.

When I asked various individuals about the Escalante affair I invariably sensed a certain uneasiness in their response. It seemed to me they would have preferred I hadn't asked the question.

No one defended Escalante; they roundly condemned him. But they insisted that the Escalante case did not involve freedom of speech or the right to criticize, rightly or wrongly. What he was sentenced for, they said, were not his ideological or political differences, but his factional underhanded methods. They were particularly incensed at what they described as his attempts to involve brother parties of other socialist countries in his dispute with the Cuban party leadership. This, they declared, could not be tolerated. They considered as criminal Escalante's determination to poison the relations between Cuba and other socialist states. Had this element not been present the entire affair would have been treated quite differently, they said.

I believe that this is an honest statement of the case, but an additional factor may have played a part. True, an organized faction was working to undermine confidence in the party's leadership and its economic policies at a critical juncture when total unity of action was required. Therefore, to organize a faction under such circumstances and to hide one's real activities from the party may be considered tantamount to treason.

Yet the question arises: Did the leadership "over-react"? Escalante could have been condemned, removed from all posts of responsibility and even expelled from the party. But should his case have been treated as a criminal one? The way in which a socialist regime reacts to internal idological differences may be of greatest importance for its future development: "over-reaction" may sometimes be as dangerous as "under-reaction." Actually, Escalante is serving his time working on a farm.

19   Accent on Youth

She was quite young, of average height and slim figure, her dark hair worn ponytail style and fastened back with a white metal clasp, such as girls and women all over Cuba wear. She was not beautiful in the conventional sense, but attractive, with clear complexion, bright twinkling eyes, and a catchy smile. She looked far too young to be the assistant principal of a boarding school, as she had been introduced to us. We learned later that she was all of 21.

This was in San Andrés, in the province of Pinar del Rio. San Andrés is a newly constructed, model farm town of some 8,000 inhabitants. It is called "model," because it was built to show farming families the cultural, social, educational and medical advantages of living in a community, rather than being spread thin over miles and miles of territory.

Before the revolution this entire Organos region had no full-time school, nor even a full-time teacher. Once a year an itinerant teacher would arrive and stay for 15 days. That was all. Now the town has two brand-new schools serving the community. One is a primary school with 1,061 children. The other is a boarding school for 300 children.

The boarding school had been opened nine months previously for children from the fourth to the ninth grades. Their average age was 14, the sons and daughters of peasants in the region. They are not handpicked nor are they above average. All that is required for enrollment is parental permission. The children stay at school for 12 consecutive days and then are taken home by bus for alternate weekends. Parents may visit every Wednesday evening and on the Sundays when their child is at school.

All the material needs of the children are met without charge. They are fed, clothed, housed; there is a school hospital, a nurse, a doctor who comes once a day, and a dentist available in town. The school has 24 teachers, including an English teacher. Each teacher sleeps in a dormitory with a group of children. In addition to the principal there is an agronomist who teaches the children scientific farming. The assistant principal also teaches.

This is typical of the boarding schools being built all over Cuba to give the children of the poorest families the best in educational facilities and to imbue in them cooperative, collective ways of thinking and high moral principles at an early age.

There is much that I could write about this particular school. But I wish to stress the fact that the oldest teacher was the 21 year-old assistant principal. All the teachers had come recently from classes at the University of Havana. This example of how young people take over major responsibilities in the new Cuba is not an isolated case. It is happening all over the island.

A new crop of Cuban youth is fast coming up behind the *barbudo* generation. They remember little or nothing of the old Cuba, but are never permitted to forget what the old Cuba was like. Nor are they likely to forget that it was young people like themselves who laid down their lives at Moncada, who went into the Sierra Maestra as boys and girls and came out two years later as mature men and women.

In Cuba the accent is still on youth. Everything is done for youth; everything expected of youth. The swankiest residential area of Havana is the Miramar section. This is where thousands upon thousands of scholarship students now live in spacious seashore residences. These students come from all over the island, especially from the homes of poor peasant and working-class people. The percentage of black youngsters is exceptionally high.

Young people also know that they now have unbounded opportunities for fully-cultured creative lives. Every field of endeavor beckons them. If they wish to be men and women of the sea, there is now a merchant marine. If they wish to be foresters, a half-billion new trees have been planted. Every branch of science, technology, medicine, pedagogy and agriculture is open to them. Only one avenue is closed. They cannot live idle, selfish lives at the expense of other people's toil.

To contrast the exciting present with the dismal past, is not to paint the present as if it were already the bright future. The young are told that the revolution is not over, but is only taking another form. The future must still be fought for; heroism and self-sacrifice are qualities that all generations must possess. The new society is built not only on material construction, but human reconstruction; old, selfish, individualistic values must be replaced by new collective ones; above all, the golden idol, Money, must be torn from its pedestal.

Another feature of the new generation is its deep feeling of responsibility for all mankind. It feels at one with the worldwide youth rebellion against imperialism and capitalism, especially with the militant youth of Latin America, Asia and Africa. When a young person joins the UJC he takes an oath to be ready to give his

life in the fight against imperialism, wherever that
might take him.

The identification of Cuba's youth with the militant
world youth upsurge is very real. It is no accident that
Cuba's daily youth newspaper, *Juventud Rebelde*, is
second in circulation only to *Granma*. Nor is it believed that rebellion is only for export; every generation is a new one and faces tasks that are somewhat
different. Always is there need for rebellion against
old habits, old prejudices and old ways of thinking that
stand in the way of the most rapid further development
of the revolution and the achievement of a communist
society. At the same time, because they are taught to
think this way Cuban youth have the highest respect
for all the positive progressive and revolutionary
traditions of the past, knowing that no generation is
weightless, suspended in space, but each standing
firmly on the experiences of the generations before it.

They also know how to enjoy life. In Havana the
young people fill the streets with the sound of their
gaiety, crowd the movies, theaters, nightclubs and
parks. They love to dance and can hold their own with
the best of U.S. youth. Rock music is very popular and
played over the radio constantly. Nor is sex a taboo
subject. It does not dominate their thinking, yet is not
treated as something to be ashamed of, but to know
and enjoy.

The most thrilling feature of Cuban youth is their
great elan, self-confidence and total commitment to
the goals of the revolution. If U.S. imperialism burned
its paws messing with Fidel's generation it will surely
burn its hide if it tries to tangle with this one.

20   Cuba and the United States

It was the United States that broke trade and diplo-
matic relations with Cuba, not the other way around;
and that, after 61 years in which the United States
humiliated Cuba and ground her under its economic
and political heel. Yet there is no hostility in Cuba toward the United States, only toward its ruling class.
Wherever I went I found warm hospitality and friendship, not only for myself as an individual, but for the
fact that I represented in their eyes another living
proof of the *other* United States—where black and
brown people fight for freedom, where workers fight
against exploitation, where young people seek a new
kind of society, and where a strong peace movement
with greater anti-imperialist understanding has arisen.

Fidel Castro has often payed tribute to the heroic
struggle of the black people of the United States. In
the speech I heard him deliver in the Plaza of the
Revolution, on the occasion of the visit of Tran Buu
Kiem, he scathingly denounced U.S. imperialism for its
bestial war of aggression in Vietnam, but had warm
praise for the struggle of the people of the United
States against the war.

There is also great interest in the internal develop-
ments of the "Movement" in the United States. People wanted to know about the Black Panther party and
about leading black personalities of whom they had
heard. They were concerned about the rifts on the Left
and the internal divisions that had arisen within the
"New Left." They wanted to know about the movement for socialism in the United States and about the
policies and activities of the Communist Party.

This solidarity with the struggle in the United States can be attributed in large part to the spirit of internationalism that pervades the Cuban air. The Cuban people follow the fight against imperialism with great sympathy, wherever it takes place. The designation of a "week of solidarity" with different countries and peoples is now a permanent feature of Cuban life. I found widespread knowledge of conditions and development in distant lands of Africa and Asia of which, to my shame, I knew little.

The special interest of Cubans in what is happening in the United States is easily understandable. The blockade continues, and as long as it does, even as its economic effects wear off, the danger of another attempt at armed invasion also continues to exist.

The Cuban people know that the survival of their revolution depends in the first place on themselves. Official Washington's hatred for revolutionary Cuba is tempered by the memory of what happened at the Bay of Pigs and by the fear that a rapacious wolf has of tangling with a testy porcupine. Washington is also aware that behind Cuba stands the Soviet Union and the other socialist countries. This too gives it good reason for pause. A factor of great importance in determining whether Cuba will be permitted to build socialism in peace or be turned into another Vietnam is the people of the United States. The Cubans know this and therefore feel a special kinship for those in the United States who struggle to make such an eventuality impossible. It must be made impossible. This is one of the great responsibilities that peace, anti-imperialist and socialist-minded people of the United States must accept, second only to ending the shameful war of aggression against Vietnam.

The Cuban Revolution is the most important event in the history of our hemisphere since the 13 colonies won their war of independence against England nearly 200 years ago. Its existence affects everything. As the Cuban people succeed in building a society in which black and brown people are the full equals of whites, its influence upon the United States will be profound. Cuba's achievements in this field have already convinced many that black and white can live and work together and that only socialism can bring this about.

During the very time I was visiting revolutionary Cuba, Governor Nelson Rockefeller was on an official Latin American mission for President Nixon. His report makes interesting reading. It admits the failure of the much touted Alliance for Progress, initiated by President John F. Kennedy with great fanfare as the U. S. reformist answer to the Cuban type of Latin American revolution. The plight of the Latin American people has not been alleviated and for many patience is rapidly running out. Even apologists for U. S. imperialist objectives and policies now admit that so-called U.S. "aid" to Latin America has been, in the words of Senator Frank Church, nothing but "an ill-concealed subsidy for American exports." Ninety cents of each dollar given in such "aid" is spent in the United States. And according to a statement made by the General Secretary of the Organization of American States, the OAS, the net inflow from Latin America was half a billion dollars for 1967 and more than two billion dollars for the first eight years of the Alliance for Progress — "In terms of net capital flow, Latin America is actually aiding the United States." More accurately stated, Latin America and its hungry, diseased and suffering people, are subsidizing the monopoly corporations of the United States.

As Cuba wins its war against underdevelopment it will have a revolutionizing affect upon all the rest of Latin America and on all other underdeveloped countries of the world. If little Cuba can do this, right next to its implacable foe and in the face of a vicious economic blockade, then there is no reason why every other country cannot also achieve full economic and cultural development.

Already Cuba is having its affects. When Peru and Bolivia begin to take over U.S. oil properties, it is because sections of the ruling class in these countries know that they can no longer argue successfully that U.S. imperialism is so all-powerful that nobody dare say it nay. When revolutionary Cuba dramatically wiped out illiteracy in one year, how can anyone defend the continued existence of mass illiteracy in other countries? When socialist Cuba wipes out polio and malaria and institutes a system of free medical and hospital care for *all* its people, who can defend the ravages of contagious diseases on such vast areas of the earth? Or, to bring matters closer to home, who can defend the shameful situation in our own rich country where millions of people cannot afford to go to a hospital, where doctor's services are outrageously high, and where the price of medicine is blown up a thousand times so that pharmaceutical firms can make increasing million in profits?

Revolutionary Cuba is a thorn in the flesh of the U.S. ruling class and that is as it should be. No one expects the mafia to make friends with those who have tossed it out on its ear and whose very example encourages other victims to do likewise. But the Cuban

Revolution is the best thing that has happened in our neighborhood. If its people can live in rent-free homes, put an end to unemployment and racial inequality, and in time come closer and closer to ending poverty, then every struggle for these ends in the United States has been strengthened, and it will be clear to all that only the capitalist system we live under prevents their realization.

Even if one does not approve of a socialist Cuba, or all that socialist Cuba does, there is still the democratic injunction that the Cuban people have the right to live under whatever economic and political system they want. It is not our business to force them to accept our own system, especially when they have already lived under it and rejected it.

To defend Cuba's right to exist as a sovereign state means to oppose the economic blockade erected around it. An economic blockade is a hostile act of war. It is imposed either as a prelude to armed warfare or as a consequence of it. It is not an act of peace, violating all precepts of peaceful relations between sovereign states. As long as it remains in force it is an indication that U.S. imperialism has not given up its intention to destroy socialist Cuba.

It should be clear to all that the blockade has failed as a measure to strangle Cuba economically. The havoc created by the shortage of spare parts for U.S.-made machines is now long past. Cubans are learning to make their own spare parts, are building their own machines or purchasing them from socialist countries and from more than a few capitalist ones. All over Cuba I saw machines from the Soviet Union, Bulgaria, Poland, Czechoslovakia, Rumania and other socialist countries, but also from Japan, England, France,

Italy and Spain. A number of capitalist countries have given Cuba long-term credits. Nothing that the United States has done or can do will stop this trend. For all intents and purposes the blockade has failed, even if it is still a nuisance, makes life more difficult for the common people, and adds to the cost of buying certain things.

The blockade has also failed in a deeper sense. It has had the opposite effect on the Cuban people from what was intended. It has become a challenge and a spur, has added to the strong national feeling that Cubans share with all people who have been oppressed, and has strengthened their resolve to carry through their revolution come what may.

At a conference of CDR activists of Matanzas province, one speaker reminded the audience of what the revolution has meant to all of them. Yes, he said, we lack many things, we do not have this and we do not have that. But there are other things we also do not have. We no longer have beggars or homeless people, nor children without school. We no longer have people without medical care, nor landless peasants, nor workers without jobs or with the fear of unemployment hanging permanently over their heads. Our cities are no longer filled with prostitutes and with corrupt politicians. No longer is there racial discrimination — we are now all brothers, all part of a single, united people. No longer do those of high society hold lavish feasts while our children and old folk die of hunger. These things our revolution does not permit. Neither are we any longer humiliated by North American imperialists or exploited by foreign monopolies. And no longer are our worker and peasant leaders assassinated. These too are some of the thing we do not have.

These things the Cuban people do not have and they will fight to the death not to have them again. That is what they mean by *Venceremos*! *Patria O Muerte*!

ABOUT THE AUTHOR

Gil Green was born in 1906, on the West Side of Chicago. During the turbulent 1930s he was national president of the Young Communist League, and served on the National Board of the American Youth Congress. For many years he has been a member of the National Committee of the Communist Party, holding various responsible posts. During the McCarthy repression of the 1950s he was convicted under the Smith Act, but remained a "fugitive from injustice" for over four years and then served an eight-year prison sentence at Leavenworth Penitentiary. He is the author of a book, *The Enemy Forgotten,* and has written many pamphlets and articles.